Dean Fraser passionately believe[s] [his] mission in life, the one thing whi[ch] right here on this plane[t] [at] [this] [time].

MY INDIGO SUN MAGAZINE

Dean shows how evolving comes from living, making mistakes which are not really mistakes but learning, walking our talk and sometimes tripping up a few times before we finally get the message about what we need in order to grow.

NEW DAWN MAGAZINE

Dean Fraser sees his mission in life to spread some much-needed laughter and love in this world

INDIE SHAMAN MAGAZINE

The sooner more know about The Thirty Second De-Stress, the sooner we can bring more peace to the world.

MORE TO LIFE MAGAZINE

Dedicated to all seekers of more than a treadmill existence. Those looking to have a fuller, happier experience on this amazing planet of ours!

Dean Fraser

THE MAGIC
OF AUTHENTIC
LIVING

Anything Possible
Is ACHIEVABLE!

Dean Fraser

2020 Copyright © Dean Fraser

Published by Alive To Thrive Ltd.

Dean Fraser has asserted his right under the Copyright, Designs and Patents Act 1988 to be identified as the author of this book and work.

All rights reserved. No part of this publication may be reproduced, stored in a retrieval system or transmitted in any form or by any means, electronic, photocopying, recording or otherwise, without the prior permission of the copyright owner.

ISBN 9781653987481

Although the author and publisher have made every effort to ensure that the information in this book was correct at press time, the author and publisher do not assume and hereby disclaim any liability to any party for any loss, damage, or disruption caused by errors or omissions, whether such errors or omissions result from negligence, accident, or any other cause. This book is not intended as a substitute for the medical advice of healthcare professionals. The reader should regularly consult their chosen medical professional in matters relating to his/her health and particularly with respect to any symptoms that may require diagnosis or medical attention.

> Love is quite simply the most powerful creative force, self-healing energy and gift to wellbeing that exists…
>
> Dean Fraser

In this life we live by our free will choice
Be quiet to listen to our own inner voice

CONTENTS

Foreword

What time is it? By the time you looked at your watch or phone it was already too late...

In the moment I asked you what time it was, that very second had already gone, therefore whatever answer you gave me had to be wrong.

The same question asked with knowledge of infinite reality can only have one answer. Now!

Now is the only possible moment.

When you started to read the line above the end of it was in your future. When you finished the line, the beginning was then in your past. You though existed in both of those moments and hopefully still do! While you were in the process of reading it, you existed only in the now. Every moment is in fact...Now.

It is the same with our bodies and the essence of us some call spirit, soul or higher self. The cells of our bodies contain a memory of everything that has happened to us and indeed an imprint for probable future events. And yet, as humans, the only possible time zone we exist in is now.

What if it were possible for us to change the way we feel about ourselves? Could we then go on to create a completely different future?

Yes!

It is indeed possible to shape our own destiny and then our life can take an entirely different direction. Through changing our mindset of what is possible from our lives, our future can then be entirely in our own hands to create whatever reality we desire. With often small changes in our daily routine and mindset, we give ourselves an amazing opportunity to enjoy a long and healthy life.

I do often have interviewers asking me how much of this stuff on authentic living that I teach do I personally use? Where am I in my own life and is every day perfect?

I am on the same journey as everyone else and can only endeavour to be the best version of myself. I fully appreciate some of these things are far easier to talk about than always practically realise. I also get that some of my wisdoms will speak to some of us more than others.

I have been on an intentional path of self-growth since the late 1980's, of course I still have life's challenges to deal with, the difference though is in perspective. Whereas once I would have see-sawed from one emotional extreme to another, these days my approach is far more centred and balanced. I attribute this directly to using the methods you will be reading about throughout our personal journey together in this book. **The book is divided into three parts.**

Part One deals with our all-important **Wellbeing & Mindset.** Covers everything we need to live an authentically holistic life. With often small changes in our daily routine and mindset we give ourselves an amazing opportunity to enjoy a long and healthy life.

Part Two choosing our perfect career though finding our personal **Labor of Love.** We deserve to enjoy our job; yet how many of us can truly make that claim? This section will show you how to reach deep inside to uncover your own personal mission in life and then give yourself permission to finally live it.

Part Three is the **Conclusion and What Next?** Once we have achieved some long-held dreams, then what? Covers consolidating your achievements so far and where to go from there…

Part One

Wellbeing & Mindset

I see them.
Seeking a bluer sky.
Those streets seemingly paved with gold.
A charmed life looked at from a distance.

What about me?
I am grateful to awaken this morning.
Another day of possibilities.
I make my reality.

Introduction

Before we go any further, we first need to address one giant elephant in the room and this is all about setting life goals...

Thinking Big Is One Way –Achievable Short-Term Goals Are Better

The reason why so many readers of books like this find themselves disappointed with the results they see manifesting in their life is mainly to do with goal setting. When they see their precious long-term dreams no closer to appearing, they conclude the author must be delusional, as they move on to the next new book to hit the shelves.

Our goals need to stretch us to become the person necessary to achieve them.

When setting any goal it is absolutely crucial to make it something we can genuinely see happening in our life. We need to be able to buy 100% into the likelihood we can achieve our goal.

So many of us unfortunately like to drift off into fantasy land when thinking about goals. "Okay, so I will have a new red Ferrari, a luxury yacht right there in the harbour at Monte Carlo and earn a billion dollars a year" now for sure this may well sound like wonderfully big thinking.

Yet if at the moment the reality is that we don't actually even hold a driving licence, have never actually seen Monte Carlo for real and earn just enough to pay the rent from our job at the local supermarket, then we are setting ourselves up for goals of disappointment.

We instead need to adopt a more step-by-step approach which will see us all the way through to attainting our current achievable goals; and allow us to set the bar continuously ever higher for the future.

I wrote my first book back in 1998, the impressively titled Unlock Your Life With Pendulum Dowsing, which I self-published. Then got on with the business of running my wholesale gift business, as the boxes containing all the copies sat gathering dust by my warehouse front door for a couple of months. One day, after tripping over one of the boxes, I asked myself my first empowering question "how can I sell these books?". The answer was clearly by making others aware the book existed. The easiest way to realise this seemed to be through directly contacting bookstores and those metaphysical shops my business already supplied to offer them opportunity to stock it. I had unwittingly also become a book wholesaler!

I set myself the initial target of wholesaling a hundred copies of my book a month. Okay, after three months into my new adventure I finally hit one hundred book sales in a month.

This prompted me to set a new target, how about I see if I can wholesale two hundred and fifty books a month? This one took a further six months to achieve. As you can imagine I was feeling pretty delighted at this point.

So, what next? Five hundred books a month seemed achievable now. Within the first year I consistently sold five hundred copies a month. I liked the way this was going!

In year two I set myself the target of selling a thousand books a month wholesale. In the end I sold ten thousand copies throughout that second year, so didn't quite reach my target of an average thousand book sales per month, yet still I felt elated. I now had solid validation people enjoyed reading my books and felt well on my way to being a long-term successful author.

Had I set out on day one expecting to sell a thousand books a month I would simply not have believed myself. I wouldn't have considered this in any conceivable way a realistic kind of goal. So when beginning my marketing for the book I would have already been self-limiting my potential.

Instead I adopted a stepping-stone mindset, setting one goal which stretched my current expectations at a time. Then another and so on. Through doing this, each time I accomplished a goal, I felt a turbo-charge of self-confidence to then expand my expectations on to a new horizon. And of course these days the bar of my expectations from book-sales is set rather higher - leading over the last decade to enjoying the kudos of ranking number one genre author five times on Amazon

Worldwide. And this can all be traced back to 1998 and aiming for those one hundred book sales a month!

Let's say you feel inspired to get fit enough to run a marathon next year, yet so far throughout adult life you haven't really taken physical fitness seriously until now. Going out for your first training run you are going to feel pretty crushed if you expect to suddenly be able to run twenty-six miles and obviously can't.

Instead you need to break-it down into attainable goals which stretch you. Set a personal target to run a mile each time you train for your first few weeks, even if this is more like a fast walk to start-off with! Then once you feel comfortable with running a mile each time, aim for two miles and so on. Right on through to finally reaching marathon ready levels of fitness a little further down the line.

Breaking down goals is an invaluable tool we have at our disposal. Setting short term targets that stretch us makes all the difference to motivation. Aiming high is great, but having achievable daily, weekly or monthly goals which stretch us ensures we keep on keeping on to ultimately reach the top. Constantly setting a new target for ourselves once the initial goal is reached.

This was essentially the secret to achieving long-term success within any goal neatly and concisely laid out right there for you in the introduction!!!

Read on to further unleash your inner potential for greatness...

Emotional Empowerment

I was once someone who found uncomfortable outwardly showing too much about how I was really feeling. At that point in my development I went through life usually wearing an impassive expression on my face, not giving too much away to others about how I really felt. Given my decision many years ago to help others to live more empowered lives, I realised how frustratingly limiting this was going to be through my interactions with audiences during talks and seminars. An inner journey became essential before I could have contemplated making the commitment to giving my first talk.

I clearly needed to radically change my approach when interacting with others and develop a new paradigm, one more congruent with my goal to spread some warmth and love during my events.

Digging down within into this defence mechanism of mine saw me uncovering this all originated from a childhood spent frequently moving schools due to my parent's careers. I had gradually stopped outwardly showing too much emotion to keep from appearing vulnerable when entering into these potentially threatening new situations; and like so many of us I still ran this obsolete programme right through into adulthood!

Using the mirror exercise described later in this chapter brought home to myself I deserved the experience of living my emotions; by outwardly showing more of what I was genuinely feeling at any given moment, others would perceive me as the authentically feeling person I really am and they would react accordingly.

From that moment I consciously adopted a habit of smiling more as I went through my day. I can confirm how this one small habit change completely transformed my relationships with everyone I interacted with. I mean this simple decision entirely changed my life!

I now love making people feel better by offering them a warm, genuine smile - to which they practically always respond in kind.

What Is False And What Is Real?

The advice I offer in my books and those I share through my talks represent my own truths as they have evolved during my several decades of experience. I would certainly never profess to possess exclusive rights to the truth. For me to expect every single word I say or write to apply to everyone I meet, regardless of their own personal story, would be overbearingly arrogant on my part.

Use those of my truths for yourself which resonate enough to feel like sound concepts to you; then see where working them can take you.

I would be foolish indeed to lay claim to be the undisputed oracle of unquestioned truth. If I ever got to feeling so egotistical I would immediately relocate to a remote small island with no means of communicating with the outside world, then I would never be tempted to share my folly with anyone else!

What Do You Think?

We all listen to this constant stream of thoughts going on in our heads. Our own inner conversation with ourselves. We identify with this voice in our head as being the true "us" and naturally automatically tend to believe everything we tell ourselves through this constant inner chatter.

Yet how can we be sure though that every single one of these thoughts or inner conversations of ours is genuinely true? Most of us believe everything we think all the time. Accepting it as concrete fact.

How about this one though?

When you were sixteen years old, assuming you are not sixteen now (and if you are sixteen "hi and kudos to you for reading this book!") did your set of belief patterns, what you were 100% sure life was really all about, match exactly with the way your belief patterns work right now?

I am going out on limb here to suggest you do not still view life in quite the same way you did at sixteen years old. Although at the time, when you were sixteen, you were so sure your thoughts were correct beyond questioning them and believed them to be the absolute truth about who you are and the world around you.

Our Truth Evolves

Learning to meditate can help a lot here. Later through our journey together meditation will duly be covered. Personally I consider this an essential life skill we can all benefit from for multi-layered reasons, not least stress management.

How many times have you gone against some inner feeling of trepidation to nevertheless forge right ahead with a course of action you kind of knew at some instinctive level did not sit quite comfortably with you? Like you I have also been there and done that. Haven't you found, as I did, that it seldom has a great outcome? All too often these rationally worked out and procrastinated decisions can turn out to be those that are catastrophic in their outcomes.

We need to opt out of believing every single conscious level thought we have, our constant inner chatter to ourselves; and automatically assuming this must be correct.

After all this is the voice which so often persuades us to maintain the safe status quo to avoid expanding our horizons.

It is these inner conversations which lead to us staying put in comfort zones, because it is easier. Well truthfully it is never easier at all, leading as it does to feelings of frustration and lack of control of our destiny. Yet so many of us do manage to convince ourselves to stay right there where we are, rather than make a leap of faith into something new, to see where saying YES takes us.

This inner chatter of ours keeps us stuck there in the same routine, trapped into running through an identical programme of thoughts and events in the same order practically every single day...the nightmare scenario.

Our inner voice can even convince us that someone we care about is deceiving us, often based on putting two and two together to unfortunately make something like twenty-seven! Do you know anyone who has ever done that? When the real facts eventually emerged, how closely did they match with what their chattering inner voice had so convinced them must be the truth?

Do you still think this inner voice of yours always has your best interests at heart?

We will do ourselves the biggest favour by instead developing a habit of trust in our intuition or gut instinct if you like. This bypasses all those ego driven conscious-level inner conversations we constantly have with ourselves and frees us to usually make the right choice.

Our imagination is one of the most powerful assets we possess. And has practically nothing whatsoever to do with logic or rational thought. It is instead listening to our intuition 100%.

Happiness Can Be A Choice

Jane felt uncomfortable with compliments or any time a significant date in her life came along, such as a birthday or anniversary, she felt overwhelmed when receiving gifts and told me she just wanted to run away from the situation. Clearly, she had underlying issues, ones which were preventing her from fully enjoying life and led to those closest around her. Jane's husband and children frustratingly failing to understand why she always reacted in such a way. Digging down into her childhood revealed she was one of six children, Jane being the middle sister of three girls. As the more responsible of the three sisters she had always looked out for her baby sister, and as there wasn't too much money around, anything Jane received over and above her basic needs being met (occasional foodie treats, gifts or new clothes) she would invariably share with her sisters.

The household was run like a military academy; with six children her parents considered imposed strictness essential for everything to run smoothly. Not surprisingly Jane felt more than a little starved of love and attention. There was a siege mentality inbred into the children, and Jane would consistently place her personal interests last to share what meagre things did come her way with her sisters.

Working with Jane over the course of several sessions got her to come to terms with her childhood and see it more in perspective. That her reality today was informed by her experiences growing-up and the guilt led feelings of somehow being unworthy of love or nice things happening for her. Forgiving her parents finally set her free. Her journey to freedom came through realising her parents were there dealing with the reality of six children, all crammed together with them in one small house, and on an extremely limited budget. As a parent herself she saw this must have been understandably stressful at times for them and imposing discipline in the way they had was just their own coping mechanism, allowing them a sense of feeling a little in control when so often they must not have felt that way at all.

Letting go of the situation through understanding a childhood situation through more informed adult eyes, and forgiving her parents, finally released Jane from her childhood guilt created emotions, to feel way more at peace when nice things happen to her now and more thoroughly able to enjoy the experience.

As we have already proven with the example of our sixteen-year-old self, our truths do continually evolve and transform. Often our inner conversations stop us in our tracks before we can ever get properly started; and yet life could be dramatically different if we just simply choose to be happy.

Poor inner conversations about happiness could sound something like this:

1. Well, you know, I need to deal with real everyday life don't I, rather than all this airy-fairy psychology stuff!
2. I am always having to pay those bills, they never seem to grow smaller, am I supposed to be happy about this?
3. Do not even start on those stressful trips to the crowded grocery store I must endure every week or any of the other thousand and one hurdles that come along in life...

4.   Life is hard and no amount of pretending it is not will make it any better!

Can you or I remain happy yet still deal with all the slings and arrows life may throw at us? Yes, for sure!

Let's go through those four points once more, instead we can choose to observe...

1.   Everyday life is where I get to test-out my ability to remain positive.
2.   I love having the money to cover my bills and so I must feel happy about being able to pay them.
3.   By being mindfully in the moment I buy-out of the collective group mind wherever I go and whatever I do.
4.   Challenges are an opportunity for me to prove to myself just what I am capable of.

Living happy is a choice, and this decision is one any one of us can make. There is a clear path to getting there which we are all free to walk.

Being happy does not mean we should adopt a Pollyanna-like attitude to ignore any of life's challenges and pretend nothing is happening. Burying our head in the sand to deceive ourselves everything is fantastically wonderful, when plainly there are issues requiring our attention, is the ultimate inauthentic way to live…

By choosing to be happily optimistic though, no matter what experiences happen along in life, we will be far more empowered to deal with it, remaining in personal control of the event. Eventually getting to the point where problems are instead viewed as challenges there to be overcome, rather than seeing them as these horrendously unfair random karmic happenings to lose sleep and worry over.

Happiness is our natural state, which is long overdue for all of us to collectively reclaim as our own.

Mirroring Smiling

Stand in front of a mirror and look closely at yourself. Pull a face that is comically glum. Next smile warmly at your reflection. Observe how this is like an instant face lift which doesn't cost a penny!

Here we are poised at the apex of an excitingly different approach to life and one which is going to unfold to be great fun (frankly, how else?).

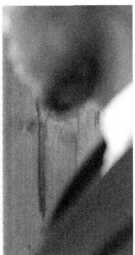

Every morning while you are looking in the mirror brushing your teeth, having a shave or doing your hair and make-up, take a few moments to look yourself directly in the eyes and smile. Make it a habit to carry on smiling for at least a minute and why not also wish yourself a happy day at the same time?

Why would you do this? Well, why not?

This exercise is useful on so many levels, on the one hand here we give ourselves permission to experience a better day. On a deeper level though, looking ourselves directly in the eyes as reflected through a mirror, does for sure eventually mirror back to us why we habitually go through life running certain programmes.

These kinds of enlightenments may take a little while to emerge, for sure though if we feel uncomfortable with showing our happy face to the world there will always be an underlying reason behind that. And as with my own experience, Mirroring Smiling will bring this issue out into the open to be finally laid to rest.

If being serious and grumpy can unfortunately often become habit-forming for so many, equally so can smiling and being happy become our habit for an empowered life. How about making smiling your new hobby? Waking in the morning, when you first open your eyes, even before you do anything else...smile.

During the day, if you sense stress mounting up to make itself known, and you are starting to feel tense, step away. Take a few moments out and go to the washroom. In privacy smile and keep it up for at least a minute, tell yourself out loud or if you prefer in your mind, that you are happy and will easily cope. Although at first it may well feel like you are acting like you are happy, eventually and surely it will soon arrive at the point where both your subconscious mind and physiology start to believe the messages of happiness they are being consistently subjected to, leading on to becoming your own wonderfully self-fulfilling prophecy.

Every time we practice active smiling not only are we re-programming ourselves to have a different outlook, but we are also creating serotonin and happy endorphins in the chemistry of our brains which act upon our nervous system...making us feel even more happy.

Triggers anchoring us to stay within happiness are useful. Here are some of those triggers, use them every day, buy-into them and watch how your attitude to life changes:

1. Smile more, it creates serotonin.
2. Find things to laugh about. Read or watch something that hits your laughter buttons; just twenty minutes laughing each day is incredibly de-stressing and youthing.
3. Are there songs or a genre of music that inspires and lifts your moods? Play them often.
4. Do you find certain colours uplifting? Wear them and surround yourself with them.
5. Walking officially lifts our moods, if you feel a little down or lethargic, go and take at least a half-hour walk.
6. Conversation and interaction with fellow positively minded humans can be incredibly uplifting.
7. As is being in love and feeling loved.
8. Spending time with our pets.

9.   Enjoy reading? Read inspiring books or stories, expanding our knowledge about something we are interested in makes us feel better.

10. Go smell a rose! Seriously, if you have a garden of your own or a local park, take the time to inhale the heady fragrance of a rose in full bloom, the scent is sure to lift anyone's mood.

11. Volunteering to help others.

12. Crosswords or mind puzzles such as Sudoku are not only calming, here we have the added benefit of brain-training as well.

It is easy to be enthusiastic when things all seem to be going well for us, how about in the more challenging times though? Those moments when there seems to be a chain reaction of all that challenging stuff happening. Then is the time to really come alive and show the world empowered enthusiasm consistently achieves goals.

Gratitude Changes Everything

It took a rock-climbing accident to open my own eyes to the power of gratitude. In the early days of my recovery, getting on with the business of regaining my full mobility, certainly put my life into focus. The simple act of walking became something I appreciated from the bottom of my heart. The same with the sea...

Allow me to explain the sea one!

Part of my self-determined journey to recovery saw me enjoying walking up to my waist in the sea, it was summer and this routine of spending around an hour each day building back my fitness, while feeling the salt water upon my body was an awesome experience. And in fact a few decades on after full recovery I still love walking in the sea.

They say that oftentimes it is a life threating or indeed in my case mobility threatening experience which opens our eyes to how amazingly wonderful our life genuinely is. Why wait for such a dramatic event to feel gratitude? There are so many things in life we can feel grateful for right now!

The Wisdom Of Gratitude

Material things do bring us temporary pleasure, but it never lasts once the newness wears off. Far better we choose to feel happy and grateful for being alive regardless of whether we have the latest smartwatch or tickets to holiday for a month vacationing in Fiji.

Okay, let's roll-out one more time for posterity the ultimate positive psychology strapline "Gratitude is the Attitude". I do get that these days this sounds like a bit of cliché, having been used so often by so many, more than likely losing most of its impact in the simplicity within which it explains an eternal truth.

And yet the paradox here is that if we do choose to practically place gratitude at the forefront of our day to day living, our life experiences will take on a whole new meaning...

Gratitude for another day absolutely attracts more things to feel grateful for. This alone ought to be motivation enough to focus on what we already have and what appreciation for it might add to our quality of life right now!

Everyone, regardless of their path through life has at least something to appreciate, and these things have often cost nothing to buy. Experiences to feel gratitude for and this might be down to even the most fundamentally basic of needs being met:

- Like clean water to drink.
- The beauty of a genuine smile given freely; I can personally attest to how this simple act changes lives.
- Looking around as the warming sun shines on down our backs or observing a beautiful cherry tree resplendently in full blossom.
- At the other end of the scale, peering out of the window at virgin freshly fallen snow yet to be walked in. As I write this it is early morning in November here in England. The crisp coolness of the night has left trees and the ground with a glistening diamond-like dusting of frost. This makes me feel thankful to be sat in my warm creative space looking out at it; and anticipating taking a walk out there a little later to enjoy the sensation of the cool cleansing air on my face.
- Witnessing a spectacular sunrise or sunset.

- An unexpectedly interesting conversation shared with a passing someone we met; and this is before we even get to thinking about friends or family, those we love or feel loved by.
- Having a place to live and a roof over our heads.
- Those life experiences which have helped shape us into the person we are today.

All the thousand and one things it can become all too easy to sort of take for granted, whereas in fact we ought to view with gratitude from the bottom of our hearts.

We need to feel able to appreciate what we already have. Passionately appreciate who we already are right now. Even though we may well possess the deepest-rooted desire to grow, we all need strong foundations to build upon - active gratitude ensures this is the case.

The only way to unlock all the magical things we have the potential for is to firstly feel grateful for what we already have and practice active gratitude every day.

Active Gratitude

Get yourself a diary, an old-school paper type, with a page for each day. This will also come in useful for some of our self-empowering exercises later in the book. For now, though let's see how to make the power of gratitude central to your daily routine, until appreciation becomes second nature.

Each morning jot down in your diary three things you can feel grateful for. Doesn't matter how small or trivial these may appear to be, and indeed how big or grand they are.

I have been practising this for many years, to give you an example, these are the three gratitude entries I wrote down for this very morning:

1. I am grateful for the cold night which has left glistening frost in its wake.
2. I am grateful for my personal library of books.
3. I am grateful to be aware enough to stay active and fit.

Of course, your entries may look entirely different. Active gratitude engenders an appreciation for nature and our own natures. Some past daily entries over the last week have seen me, amongst other things, being grateful for trees, the gift of sight, freedom to be me, meditation, the beautiful sky one morning, being a wordsmith and even gratitude for feeling gratitude!

Let active gratitude become second nature and watch the transformation happen in your life. Make it your habit when first waking up to be genuinely thankful for another day and the opportunities it is surely going to bring.

While you are looking in the mirror in the morning (that early morning bathroom mirror again, for sure this is the most effective moment to programme how your day will unfold) look yourself in the eyes taking a moment to think of all the things you can feel grateful for. This can be down to the most fundamental of your needs being met, like the fact you even have the mirror to gaze into and a bathroom with instant access to water (when so many around the world could only dream of such luxury).

Then write the feeling down in your diary. Our diary then becomes our personal motivational book. If we ever feel challenged by life circumstances, we can look back over all the daily gratitude entries in our diary, to motivationally remind us of who we really are, and how we appreciate life. Invaluable when we need to keep on keeping on all the way to dealing with that challenge and laying it to rest.

Make it fun and enjoy feeling grateful. If you can laugh and smile all the better, positive emotions carry the message of gratitude infinitely stronger. And the personal energy we put out there into the universe is what makes our life.

We want to be constructing our own life how we desire it rather than events controlling us...gratitude goes a long way to making this real for us.

The more we can express our thanks and gratitude for what we already have...the more we allow greater and more outrageously wonderful experiences to enter our lives. Bringing us the naturally occurring self-fulfilling prophecy of appreciably feeling even more gratitude.

What have you got in your life to be grateful for? Find something. Find lots and lots of things! And really express that gratitude!!!

Feel The Love

"Love can be a verb and a noun, and sometimes an abstract noun" so much for the dictionary description...

Love is quite simply the most powerful creative force, self-healing energy and gift to wellbeing that exists.

Whatever achievements we wish to accomplish, if they are worthy of our precious time and energy, deserve to be invested with a large healthy dose of love. Love for what we are doing turbo-charges the transformational energy permeating right throughout our reality, ensuring any desired changes are massively more likely to manifest.

Love invested in our actions means we are absolutely trusting in what we are doing. Here is something which we are showing to ourselves and the universe truly matters! We are making a resolute commitment to see this all the way through to its conclusion for the long-term awesomeness it brings into our life...

Our Happy Point

Love is the most powerful motive force for manifestation of our goals in the Universe. **Self-love is essential if we hope to gain mastery of the game of life.**

The following exercise will begin the flowering of self-love within your heart. Please be sure to read through all the steps before starting the exercise:

1. To plant the smallest acorn of self-love to grow into your inner oak tree of certainty, you need to find somewhere you will not be disturbed for the next twenty minutes. Sit in a relaxing chair or lay down if that feels more comfortable, as you start to concentrate all your attention solely on your breathing. Observe how your body feels, is there any tension anywhere? Gently move your shoulders or any other tense area of your body to release that tightness, as you continue to centre attention completely on your breathing.

2. You are going on an inner journey deep into your essence to discover your Happy Point.

3. Gently ponder all the many facets making up your uniqueness as the person you are. Relaxing into the sensation, choose to focus on one part of who you are which you feel happy with. And it doesn't

matter how small or seemingly unimportant this single facet may appear to be. One brilliant fraction of all that makes up the whole of you, which works so well for you and always makes you feel at ease within and happy. One selected piece of the myriad of you which sits so beautifully with you that would never wish to change it in any way.

4. Enjoy the warmth of the emotion as you concentrate all your attention entirely on how this wonderful part of you makes you feel when you think to feel deeply about it. Spend at least five minutes keeping the thought, the feeling, central to your feelings.

5. Next you need to apply a colour to that feeling. It does not matter what colour that might be, one which just seems right to your intuition is the perfect choice. This wonderful feeling now imaged together with your Happy Point colour of choice...spend some time strongly visioning this colour as you bask in the warmth of the feeling.

6. Let's see how you can bring that warm feeling into other parts of your life and begin to transform through love. I mean wouldn't it be amazing to feel this fabulous across the entire spectrum of the rainbow of you? Let's make this happen...

7. Still focussing deeply on the amazing feelings associated with this part of you that feels wonderful, now seen together with the colour this feeling is associated with...slowly begin to re-align your attention to instead think about some other aspect of yourself that you sense needs some definite work. Maybe this can be something you dislike in your own reactions to situations or a habitual pattern of thinking you empathically know has outlived its time.

8. It is important here to only concentrate on the one area you sense needs work for this session.

9. As you ponder how all the emotions associated with this more challenging part of you makes you feel, gradually overlay this feeling with the **colour** you associated with those beautiful, warm feelings you experienced a few moments ago. All you can now see in your mind is your Happy Point colour. Feel this! *You deserve to really feel this!!!*

10. You can return to your normal waking state when you sense you have done enough for this session.

What is happening here is the start of an inner transformational process. You are self-healing to welcome self-love into your life. Re-programming old issues through healing them once and for all. And feeling far more comfortable in your own skin and accepting of who you are.

We all have choices on which paths to take in life, we are constantly presented with potential directions we can take. And now you possess your own personal map to self-love take the time to follow it.

We are all perfect at being ourselves, we just need reminding how. Then our higher-self, and through this our connection to source, grows stronger through every day of our life.

Any time we find ourselves facing a challenging situation or tackling a potentially toxic person, if we recall and stay focussed on the colour associated with our Happy Point, we bring love into the situation. And nothing is more empowering than love!

You might even like to reinforce this process further by wearing or keeping the colour you associate with your Happy Point around your immediate environment.

The more you practice this the easier it gets, and a natural part of the process is you experience the beginning of a transformed approach and outlook to life unfolding for you.

Daily Empowerment Routine

As we already established, in the morning it is incredibly self-empowering to take a few minutes to think of a few things you can feel some passionate gratitude for...which helps keep that feeling with you throughout your day.

Last thing at night you can do the same, focus your attention on your goals as you fall asleep. This is programming your subconscious mind to work for you on your behalf. To afford you the life experiences that YOU need and attract all those things into your day which help you travel all the way to authentic living becoming your reality.

We need to build a new paradigm from the ground up...

Let Construction Commence

Building a house to stand the test of time begins with firm foundations, it is precisely the same with building a future full of personally inspiring new ideals. Only once the foundations are in place, and in our case this would be having established what we genuinely want from life and how exactly our perfect lifestyle looks, then the real construction can commence. Then arrives the exciting part when we step right ahead to see where this journey will take us.

In our information technology driven world we are easily able to instantly access the answer to virtually any question about practically anything or research the background to whichever person we want to know more about, all right there at our fingertips. Inevitably this can lead us to also sometimes expect these similar kinds of instant results from our lives. For sure we can find ourselves in brilliant new adventures by developing the habit of saying YES to those unexpected opportunities which come our way, however, the truth is that the process of building a completely new lifestyle from the ground up does require dedication and persistence.

Positive changes will never require us slogging away to the detriment of enjoying life. On the contrary we need to ensure when fulfilling long term goals of any kind, be they improving our health or venturing onto exciting new career paths, that these genuinely improve our quality of day-to-day life.

The only way our goals stand the best chance of manifesting for us is if we feel happy each day throughout the process of making them happen...

Let Life Teach You

If we have consistently done things one way and then suddenly shift our entire intentions this will usually take a little while to show-up in our life.

Think of it like going off to university, here though the lecture hall becomes your own life experiences.

You would hardly expect to qualify as a doctor in three months, becoming proficient at taking control of your own life is precisely the same. Mastery comes through experience. Learning opportunities will be encountered.

You are educating yourself and your ongoing life is the lecturer.

Every time we become aware of and leave behind any deeply entrenched mindset, one we have for far too long bought-into which might have limited our ideal lifestyle from existing, we are placing ourselves so much closer to this ideal lifestyle's permanence.

Accept The Gift

What if a person you are loosely acquainted with, from the outer edge of your extended circle of friends totally out of the blue offered you an all-expenses paid holiday of your choice? All you needed to do was pick the destination and then turn up at the airport on the day, how would you react?

How about a distant second cousin randomly deciding to gift you a new car? What then?

Moving closer to home, how do you feel when your temporarily unemployed friend insists he wants to stand his round of drinks at the bar or you receive an unexpectedly generous birthday present from your elderly relative who relies only on her pension to live?

With the law of energy or chi taken into consideration there can be only one response. Smile as you graciously accept the gift and be happy for the generosity of the perpetrator, for surely their actions in due course are about to bring about many good happenings into their own life. To react in any other way we are treating ourselves like we are somehow unworthy of good things happening.

We always deserve good things happening in our lives. Irrespective of what we may have always thought to the contrary. It is our birthright to deserve to feel good...be happy!

We need to allow for the good flow of energy. Any freely offered gift needs to be accepted with peace and grace.

This is our role in the transaction. And this can equally take the form of the gift of someone giving of their time, listening to us rather than talking. This opportunity also must be cheerfully accepted and with due gratitude. Any other course of action would be interrupting the giver's personal energetic flow of attracting good things via the actions of their own energy and you or I certainly don't have the right to do any such a thing.

Always feel comfortable with accepting a freely offered gift and develop the habit of feeling infinitely happy for the giver's generosity. Knowing that for sure it will boomerang straight back into their life at some point and probably soon.

Why not also get into the habit of freely giving kindness to others for creating mini miracles in your own life?

Instant Confidence

The way we present our physiology to the world reveals precisely how we view ourselves. And anyone who understands even the fundamentals of body language will be able to pick up on these signals.

Through our posture we lock-in how we feel, this indicates our current emotional state and level of self-esteem. And yet we can make the choice to transform all this in a moment. We can do this right now and the effects are immediate.

This takes us far beyond basic body language, directly into using our own physiology to create the moods we want to experience and powerfully feeling in control.

We have an amazing lever at our disposal here and it really is practically so simple that you could well initially have difficulty in accepting it can make such a radical difference in your life. It does...

This is one of the most popular subjects I cover in my talks, once my audiences get what a radical transformation our physiology can make in how they feel and are perceived by the world. Typically, at my events I demonstrate three models of physiological behaviour - starting with a political candidate looking to be elected, next a supermodel strutting her stuff down the catwalk and finishing off with a habitually dishonest salesperson. These comedic representations of physiological archetypes serve to illustrate the point in a way which usually stays with my audiences (and apparently also demonstrates I am quite happy to look a little silly in the name of our greater understanding!).

Applying your physiology to work for you through transforming your happiness, confidence and integrity is 100% experiential. Once you have put this into practice for yourself, you will get how powerfully this works.

Smile More

Release that serotonin and you start to feel better almost immediately, and others will gravitate towards you more. Remember this simple game-changing trick; smiling makes anything we need to deal with seem a little easier.

Genuine laughter is free and changes moods in a moment.

Look Up

If we are feeling down we also tend to walk around looking down at the ground. Want to feel instantly better? Look up! What could be simpler?

Rather than staring down at the ground or a mobile phone screen while walking or indeed sitting, instead look upwards towards the horizon. Pay attention to the architecture way up there at the top of buildings, see those things higher up in the landscape many people miss through waking around looking at their own feet. Raise your gaze to look at trees, birds in flight and the pattern of clouds in the sky. Develop this habit to feel more positively happy (but still be sure to look where you are walking!).

Open Gestures

Any gesture where we fold our arms across our body is protective (unless we are cold or in pain when we fold our arms to keep heat in or hug ourselves for comfort). Same with habitually having hands stuck in our pockets, this is also protective, and others will intuitively pick up on this signal. We can kick this self-limitation into touch instantly to raise our internal confidence barometer! I have not folded my arms for well over two decades (seriously).

By avoiding folding our arms and keeping hands out of pockets, once we get over the strangeness of this new habit, we do genuinely start to feel far more confident and personally empowered.

Posture

How we stand, our posture, affects the way we feel.

Take the time to observe any successful person you admire as they interact out there in the big wide world. How do they stand and walk? How is it different from your posture and walk? Chances are, whatever their physical size, they stand up straight and walk tall – meaning their posture is upright, shoulders back as they squarely look the world in the eyes. Mirroring this walking success story to adjust your own stance and walk will pay instant dividends in terms of the way it makes you feel powerfully more confident.

Seated Posture

At home feel free to loll away in your favourite chair. In the workplace or when attending business meetings we come across as far more engaged if our posture is upright (but not rigid) with our head facing in the general direction of whoever is doing the talking. I know that might seem almost too obvious, that we need to look at the person talking, believe me I have been in front of enough audiences over the years to easily observe who is genuinely engaged in what I am saying and those who are more interested in what they might grab for lunch in the intermission!

Paying attention means we are mindfully engaged right there in the moment; others will notice and respect our opinion far more. We will also tend to remember what was being said, which is always useful.

Shaking Hands

We have all met those bone-crushers who shake hands like they are taking part in some sort of iron man style power contest. We also know this truthfully makes them look anything but powerful, instead they come across as just a little bit immature. At the other end of the scale we have experienced those who shake hands like a damp dishcloth, while failing to make any eye contact.

The happy balance here is a firm handshake, while making eye contact and then let go. We come across as business-like and confident, happily re-enforcing us feeling more business-like and confident.

Face Touching

Typical gestures of a liar are nose, mouth or eye scratching, ear rubbing (their own, not yours!) and shifting around within their stood or seated position. If we witness at least a few of these gestures from someone chances are they are being economical with the truth.

If you find yourself often using these gestures you might want to look at ways to improve your choice of words to communicate with more credibility and get your opinions listened to. Anyone who consciously avoids face touching gestures or shifting around when talking will find themselves quite automatically communicating in an entirely different way, with some real integrity.

Physiology Summary

Taking on board these physiological gifts for yourself is such an easy and instant way to transform your life as you apply them. The positive results we get are always the most convincing validation of anything we adopt which is new.

Combining positive physiology with the right mindset awakens our inner genius...

Transforming Your Life Starts With You

Kevin had two tasks in life he derived no pleasure from at all and they had genuinely begun to make him feel overwhelmed as he didn't see how he might avoid them. A successful builder, he recently acquired a beautiful house with an equally beautiful expansive lawned garden and Kevin disliked mowing grass with a passion. As an inherently practical hands-on kind of guy it had literally never crossed his mind to employ the services of a landscape gardener to take care of it all for him.

Now with one task which made him feel unhappy out of the way and sorted, next we needed to address the main source of his stress. This was the one which sometimes kept him awake all night. Namely dealing with the financial book-keeping for his business. Starting out years ago as a sole trader, as his company grew to employing over twenty tradespeople, so had Kevin's headache about keeping his accounts records up to date. Again, his mindset had yet to catch up to his success!

I suggested to Kevin his time would be better served supervising his team and getting out giving quotes to gain potential new clients; and this would be palpably easier for him if he employed the part-time services of an accounts clerk for a few days a week to take care of all the booking-keeping, invoicing and admin for his business.

Two overwhelming burdens from his life removed by passing across those tasks he loathed to other people who enjoyed them! Win/win.

Focus on what you enjoy doing and if at all possible delegate or pass across those tasks you personally find unremittingly boring or simply have no talent for, to someone who is rather brilliant at them and has fun doing what you dislike.

Over To You

Any of us can make the choice right now to change things to become more empowered, to live a more authentic lifestyle.

The greatest martial artists practice controlled power – here is true empowerment. Any martial arts practitioner who uses only unchanneled aggression or worse still

anger, is unlikely to stay the course. And it is precisely the same for us when we walk the path of our greatness.

It really is genuinely possible for any one of us to take the decision to live an authentically real life. Never has the phrase, life is all about the attitude, been more relevant.

Live authentically and you can expect to:

- Nurture trust on your intuition – it will not always seem to make logical sense to follow your gut instinct, but all of us would be wise to develop this habit.
- Invest all your actions with unceasing amounts of passion and remain adaptable within your approaches along the way to ensure success, but still authentically true to your own personal life-plan.
- Develop a personally empowered mindset, committing to see plans through to their conclusion.
- Expect those you meet will have entered your life for a reason. To help you or them to grow into the person necessary to manifesting goals.
- See the opportunities in life's challenging situations, those ones so many others do miss.

- Staying mindfully in the moment to ensure maximum effectiveness.
- Controlling the direction of your personal future by setting targets and finding ways to take some kind of action every day (however small) to achieve them.
- Realising how a few simple adjustments in lifestyle can dramatically reduce stress and the likelihood of developing serious health issues.

Not everything is going to go as smoothly as we anticipated every single day, this happens to allow us to learn. An empowered mindset ensures we keep on going anyway and never get distracted or give away personal power by starting to feel sorry for ourselves. The best way to improve our reality is to take personal responsibility for our own life and then get out there to make those changes we want for ourselves.

Anyone, no matter who they are or what circumstances they might currently live in, can turn things around to make their life more empowered and live a more authentic lifestyle...

Buy Into It 100%!

Buying into your own goals allows others to as well...

If you want your ideas and goals to get taken seriously, the candid truth is YOU need to be the one to take them seriously first.

1. How important to you are those changes you want to make in your own life?
2. Are they a priority?
3. Can you get passionate about them?
4. Do YOU believe in your own goals being achievable?
5. Will you carry right on until you achieve them?
6. What are you prepared to do to help yourself?

Walking the path to personal achievement with others also buying into your vision of how amazing life really is increases the fun factor tenfold. Lending much appreciated extra supportive energy throughout the process of getting there. Most self-made people will have a network of mentors behind their success. Yet they may never have even met some of them!

We thankfully have access to the wisdom from any book, videos and audio downloads to help us on our journey...

Caring Enough

If we do not care how is anyone else supposed to care either? It might seem like the easiest choice in the world to not care, after all we are never going to be disappointed if we decide nothing matters.

Yet…and yet what do we set ourselves up for here?

The paradox here is that by not caring we are setting ourselves up for disappointment after disappointment, until unfortunately this becomes kind of the accepted normality for us. Learned helplessness.

I met a woman a few years ago at one of my talks who told me "I am an eternal pessimist and I always expect the worst-case scenario from anything new". I asked her how that life-plan was working out for her and she told me she is constantly disappointed with life. And this could all be so different for her! At the point, when we talked, she wasn't yet ready to change her philosophy. Perhaps she will read this book and it will finally allow her to love life rather than hate it? I hope so.

Caring about our own life, our destiny, requires commitment. Life will inevitably still present challenges (this is how we grow as people) yet caring will ensure we find a way around, over or even through the issue before us. And the reason is because we dare to care. We are personally invested in the process of creating our own amazing reality.

Would you rather opt to remain passive as you observe everyone else moving on in life and having all the fun? Or choose to be right there in the driving seat of your own life? Being the one making awesome experiences happen for yourself...

Free-will dictates everyone always possesses these options. I know which I prefer and my whole motivation through my writing and delivering talks is showing others those choices. Offering my readers and audiences the option to take self-empowerment over inaction.

What we focus our attention on creates our reality every moment. Constantly attempting to monitor the myriad of the millions of those abstract thoughts we have each day is impossible and quite likely the fast-track road to madness!

What we can all do though is remain vigilant to any self-limiting patterns in our thoughts which might be us attempting to persuade ourselves, with poorly conceived reasons, to stay right where we are. Buying into an excuse for inaction rather than actively engaging with life.

Helpful Thoughts

What we consistently think about affects firstly our own self-image and consequently how we are then perceived by others. Our thoughts (and words) also directly influence our actual physical wellbeing and mental health.

The cells of your body and mind, every single moment of every single day, are bombarded with thoughts and more crucially the emotions felt behind those thoughts. We have the thoughts of ourselves and like it or not, also the thoughts of those around us. And our bodies and minds will listen to these messages and words it receives loud and clear, reacting accordingly – regardless of our conscious awareness of it.

We create our personal version of reality through thoughts. What we think, feel, and say is played forward as the reality of our life.

Yet if we care to listen to those words of others when they voice opinions about us to our face, to a greater or lesser degree these validations of how they see us or the kind of life we ought to be leading, can affect our inner and outer well-being. All depending quite literally upon how much credence we give to their point of view!

Our health, happiness and financial reality are all reactions to the messages we are constantly sending out about ourselves and receiving from others.

This energy helping us to become our own walking talking living breathing manifestation of how exactly we ought to look and the life we should lead. For better or unfortunately all too often for worse!

For sure this can all be different though...radically different. That word **choice** comes into play once more.

Through much of our journey together my goal is specifically aimed at breaking down any of your unconscious self-limitation habits - to instead place you right there in the pole position of deciding where your life goes.

It seems almost too obvious to state that feeling good about YOU is vital for happiness and living beyond any possible self-imposed limitation! Yet many of us do run programmes forward into our lives which achieve anything but that desired outcome.

Think of people you know. Do those who moan and complain all the time come across as brilliantly happy examples of humanity?

Or the professional cynic, expletively going through life mocking others and exhibiting sarcasm, do they seem full of joy?

Are those who fixate on illness usually healthy?

At the other end of the scale, how about those teachers at high-school who always seemed to have a ready smile and were encouragingly inclusive with the pupils in their class, perhaps you met at least one of these educational gems on your journey through school? These teachers rarely had to discipline students as they were all too engaged with learning, and everyone felt better for attending their lessons. Or how about the neighbour who is genuinely interested in what we have to say, never gossips, and laughs along with our jokes, don't you feel good for passing a few moments with them? These guys are happy people, sure they have their share of issues like all of us, yet they choose to face the day with a smile and pleasant words.

Focussing And Acting On What We Actually Want

If I would love to be a scratch golfer, sitting there each day chanting affirmations *"I am grateful to be a scratch golfer"* yet taking absolutely no personal action myself to achieve this goal will never automatically make me go around the course in par. How I can make it work though is if I firstly take the time to study and carefully mirror the mindset of a professional golfer I admire. Then as perfectly as possible replicate their playing techniques to make it all real. I do then incrementally increase the chances that I will genuinely soon enjoy being that scratch golfer!

The subconscious mind acts like a data storage file for all our experiences.

And we constantly programme our subconscious through our consistent thoughts, words and actions. We are our own self-fulfilling idea of exactly how we should look and shape of the future life experiences we will have. And every one of us constantly does this completely regardless of whether we are ever aware of the fact.

Yet We Have A Choice

Our mindset is 100% in our own hands. We can think whatever we choose...

Rather usefully our freedom of choice means that we can go right ahead right now to mould our own life for ourselves, choose how we learn from our experiences. Reclaiming our personal power to take charge of shaping our future destiny by simply choosing exactly what we centre our conscious thoughts on. Programming our subconscious constructively rather than unintentionally limiting our capacity for greatness.

And as we have already established, our subconscious minds are consistently programmed with our own conscious thoughts anyway and more alarmingly also with the thoughts of those around us if we care to listen to their opinions about who we are or what we ought to do in our life.

It is all too easy to lose track of our own motivations, personal standards and authentic self, if we pay too much attention to the constant stream of words coming our way from even well-meaning family and friends, never mind about those toxic people we all encounter from time to time!

(Dis)Comfort Zones

Public speaking had already become second nature to me, I felt (and still do) a buzz of excitement of pure joy stood before an audience ready to communicate. This will always be an inherently two-way communication. I know my own story inside out; I prefer to know yours and then I might help you more effectively. I often get asked if I feel nervous before giving a talk. Never, I love what I do and standing in front of an audience open to learning life-transforming techniques is an amazingly life-affirming experience. I never work from scripts. I trust when I get up to talk that I will automatically have the words to impart the points I wish to cover; and because of this every event sees me adapting my subject matter once I begin to sense what will work best for this particular audience. As with my writing, I feel my role as a public speaker is to mainly get out of my own way to allow the relevant information to reach my readers and audience through me.

Poetry was an altogether different proposition.

The prospect of laying myself creatively on the line, publicly sharing my poetry for the first time did lead me to question my sanity more than once as the date of the evening literary festival approached. I felt compelled to go ahead regardless though, if only to walk the talk once again and live the message I have been sharing with others for years about the leaving of our comfort zones.

As I arrived at the venue on the night in question the organiser came to see me backstage and asked me for a favour. Having attended one of my 100% Naturally Stress-Free Events, he already knew how I usually function in front of an audience and so he asked if I might mentor three nervous first-time performance poets and let them share the stage with me, then they would feel more at ease. He assumed, as a regular on stage I knew what I was doing and equally assumed that I must have performed poetry many times before. All my own concerns forgotten, of course I said YES to his request.

And us four went on stage together that night, standing next to one another at microphones, with me there in the middle to lend them a little extra sense of security. I introduced us, performed a poem, then led my new friends through their own performances, each of us taking it in turns to share our creative endeavours. It was brilliant fun and for the hour we had been allotted I believe we managed to entertain our audience. Well they applauded when we reached the end and before that laughed at the right moments, so chances are they enjoyed our poetic tales.

Ironically the organiser did me a great favour that night without knowing it. He placed me straight into a mindset I felt 100% comfortable with. Mentoring others, helping them to find the inner confidence to leave their comfort zones, resulted in me not even considering my own anymore. After all mentoring is my stock-in-trade, it is what I do! My own misgiving completely forgotten, out I went personally feeling like I had been performing poetry for years and that is exactly how everyone perceived me.

Mindset is everything and the apparent limitation of a comfort zone might well turn out to have been a mirage after all once you and I choose to do something awesome and embrace one of those slightly scary new experiences.

Thought patterns get hard-wired into the neural pathways in our brains. The more we practise something the better we get at doing it. Yet, unfortunately not all these neural pathways work in our own best interests. They become a self-limiting way of life and usually it takes a wake-up call for us to transform away from these patterns and form a new neural pathway or paradigm.

The Third Thought

For most people their thought processes, those inner conversation going on through their conscious minds goes something along these lines:

THOUGHT ONE A brilliantly original idea or concept spontaneously appears out of nowhere. Maybe it is there when they awaken one morning; perhaps observing something in passing opens their eyes to a hitherto unseen opportunity or a conversation suddenly inspires them to see the world in an entirely new way. Naturally they feel engaged and excited at this point.

THOUGHT TWO Okay, so next to do something with this amazing inspiration. For a short while their mind works overtime on different positive ways this idea can now happen for real. Practically getting from where what at the moment is only the idea, carrying on all the way through to its magnificent realization consumes their attention full-time.

THOUGHT THREE They gradually begin having an inner conversation of limitation. Helping them to find some valid (and poor) excuses for inaction. Next they persuade themselves how it would all be far more sensible to not really have this happen anyway. Their newly formed excuses convincing them that this was all a terrible idea after all. Far better to stay put right there in their safe comfort zone (trapped) because this is always the easier option.

We have all just witnessed a comfort zone in action. Sadly, this mindset single-handedly stops more potential winners from achieving their goals than anything else. How many incredibly pioneering inventions or life changing innovations have been lost to comfort zone self-limitation we will never know.

It bears repeating that repetition creates habits, this fact can be invaluable when opting to move our life forward.

The more we do something new the more we lock-it into ourselves and then gradually it becomes second nature to act or think within this new paradigm.

It is precisely the same with those old, entrenched comfort zones – we hold so tightly onto them precisely because we have always thought or done things that way. And yet we have always possessed the freedom to live beyond comfort zones. Effectively by-passing all those inner conversations that we run through our minds, those self-justifying excuses for inaction.

In fact, only possessing the knowledge of the existence of these inner conversations of limitation goes a long way towards reducing their power over us. Through this awareness we can recognise them for what they are when faced with any moments of decision making and choose to buy-out of running those old programmes once and for all.

Loving To Pay Tax

Back in my early days in business a few decades ago each year I would take myself miserably off to my accountant when it came the designated time to file my annual accounts, and each time for sure I dreaded being informed the amount of tax I found myself burdened with needing to pay that year. It never grew smaller; in my mind it seemed to me I was working hard in my business to fund the tax office and keep all those guys employed. Dave, my accountant would usually shrug his shoulders and remind me to pay my tax before the due date.

One particular year along came that dreaded tax-time again, only for me to discover Dave had promptly taken early retirement due to poor health. I needed to find a new accountant and fast!

A recommendation led me to Amanda; recently having left one the big accountancy firms, to set up in practice for herself. Her advert tagline went something along the lines of 'Innovating New Approaches To Accountancy'. I liked the sound of this and duly made an appointment.

Bringing along my accounts files for Amanda to look over, during the meeting I mentioned my usual grievance about how each year since I started in business I needed to pay more tax and how I felt I was working for the government.

She looked over her glasses across the desk at me. *"Dean, I love having to pay more tax each year, this means I must be becoming more successful each year and if I am earning a higher percentage of profits annually then I have to be doing things right. My taxable income increasing year in year out is what motivates me as I know my turnover is heading in the right direction!"*

Okay, this one took a few moments to sink-in. I suppose I must have looked a little shocked as I sat there for at least a minute staring and feeling temporarily speechless.

In one short statement Amanda had managed to entirely transform my belief patterns regarding paying tax. Given me a new paradigm.

Before then my mindset and thoughts had been focused entirely on the 35% (or whatever it literally was at the time) of everything I earned needing to be given to the government in tax and increasingly resenting when each year this amount grew. From that moment on I loved paying my tax, especially if it turned out to be significantly higher than the previous tax year. I knew if this happened I must have equally significantly increased my profits that year.

A friend recently stated that if he worked overtime at the weekend he would have to pay 40% in tax on everything he earned. I suggested he would be wiser to look at this as earning 60% more than if he hadn't done the overtime. Given his grumpy *"I suppose so"* response I am not sure he is quite ready yet to buy-into my proffered different way of looking at his reality.

How we chose to look at life ensures the experience we will have in that same life.

A comfort zone is very much like an old favourite jacket, it is a little shabby and doesn't look so cool these days yet carries on being worn because it feels comfortable.

Although many of us do for sure initially have every intention of carrying through a plan or working towards fulfilling a long-held goal, unfortunately for the majority of people it does not quite end up playing out like that. We end up buying into Third Thought excuse making instead...

Excuses Won't Cut It Anymore

Some hold onto the excuse "it's just my karma" to validate their reasons for remaining static, they feel this is a good enough reason to stay exactly where they are. To be blunt, this is a poor excuse for inaction.

And my word there are so many more awful personal excuses for inaction!

Proclamations along the lines of:

- "Oh well, you know nobody in my family ever achieved much so I guess I'm just going to accept that I won't either"
- "I tried further education years ago when I left school as a teenager and when it didn't work-out I felt like a failure, I'm sure never going to study anything new again"
- "It's not my fault I wake every day lacking in any energy and motivation, it's just my genes"
- And then we have the classic "I'm too young, old, short, tall, unqualified, overqualified, beautiful, unattractive, unconventional, shy (delete as appropriate)!"

Every single one of these are frankly garbage excuses to now throw right into the trash where they belong!

Before we leave excuses I absolutely need to share with you this one extra special gem of an excuse that I had said to me a few years ago and in all seriousness "well you know, I would love to stop smoking cigarettes, but I meditated on this and I now know God intends for me to be a smoker". This woman really felt she had come up with the ultimate validation to keep right on doing things the way she always had. I mean what an excuse! Wow!!!

The Easiest Way To Leave A Comfort Zone

This applies equally if we are afraid of going for promotion, dating, public speaking, visiting the dentist, travelling to another country, ballroom dancing, mountain climbing, spiders, reading a book, getting physically fit, having our own business, further educating ourselves, skiing, writing a CV and any of the thousand and one things which can cause us to break-out into a cold sweat at the prospect of.

Is there something you might have always wondered what it was like to do but your self-imposed comfort zone limitations seemingly rendered this impossible?

If you live with a phobia think about when you first really experienced it, where in your personal history did you become aware of this reaction? What age were you?

If you have a fear of spiders, as a small child did you witness someone else reacting in fear at the sight of a spider?

Same with a fear of flying, perhaps you once saw photos in a newspaper or saw an incident on television what featured a plane crash? Maybe you even overheard a conversation or documentary questioning the safety of flying.

Since quite early childhood I had possessed an irrational terror of large ships. Even seeing one in movie or documentary was enough to trigger sheer panic within me. Eventually, as an adult I decided it was time to do some tracing back through my own timeline to find the cause. After recalling when I first felt this way about ships, I realised this all originated from a children's picture book I had glanced through in year one of school (when five years old!) about Titanic and other shipwrecks. These images became lodged in my subconscious and "protected" me from ever going near a ship, so I didn't end up sharing the same fate as those people I saw in the child's picture book. Crazy as this all sounds, for sure my story does mirror those of many others who go through life fearing certain experiences or even objects, with no real knowledge of why this might genuinely be.

Finally, about twenty years ago I chose to undertake a daytrip on the very source of my fear. A large passenger ferry for a day trip to visit France. In quite rough seas as it turned out to be on the day – only to leave myself with no other alternative but to have to repeat the same journey in reverse (in even rougher seas!) coming back home later that day in the evening. This experience sure cured me of that one once and for all!

And you can do the same with anything similar in your own life to mentally tick off another supposedly impossible task completed...

The most effective way to leave any comfort zone is to walk right ahead towards whatever is limiting you. Confront that inner demon. Tweak it on the nose a bit. Face your fear head on; and then actually go ahead and do it!

I can promise you the feeling is incomparable, the boost to self-esteem and confidence is worth all the temporary pain and angst. Better still you have permanently removed another barrier from your life.

To change life for the better quite literally all that is needed is a shift in awareness of what can really be brilliantly possible and then consciously choosing to go out there to make that possibility your reality.

This simple shift in belief about what is possible becomes emphoweringly transformational. Overcoming comfort zones places your future directly into your own hands, then any changes you choose are measured and intentionally carried through by YOU!

Do Something Different Each Day

Routine is a killer to ambition. Repeating the same pattern day in day out puts us into a passive mindset of limitation. Doing something different each day rather usefully places us instead there into the empowered mindset of accepting our life can also be different.

Doing something different can seem trivial yet pay incalculable dividends in terms of our adaptability to new situations.

Something different can be as small as:

- Driving past the usual slot here we always park our car, to go and park someplace else on the car park.
- Taking an even slightly different route on the same journey we habitually do every weekday.
- If we always head left out of the door from our place of work to go buy a bagel for lunch, turning right to sample something we have not had before.
- If we constantly wear black, putting on a red top today.
- Reading a book or doing crosswords rather watching television for one evening.
- Going to the opera one mid-weekday or indeed any of the millions of other small variations in our daily

routine which lead us into experiencing new unchartered waters.

Getting into the habit of doing something different each day will usefully also make dealing and coping with any unexpectedly stressful situations considerably easier for us.

Committing to even one small change in daily routine ensures our subconscious becomes habitually used to variety, then as we gradually leave behind any limiting discomfort zones, positive change happily becomes our expectation from life.

Does Your Instinct Say It's Right? Then It Usually Is...

After a decade or so of working successfully in one form or another within the business world, I took time out from my career for an entire year. I learned meditation, travelled to visit ancient sacred sites, built up my library and networked with fascinating people who were also exploring and experimenting with human potential. Having quit my well-paid job I lived off savings, taking the opportunity to explore within both myself and human potential. Some people thought I was mad; I knew I was right!

Avoid clinging on to any situation which is clearly intended to be part of the past. Let it go. Seek pastures new, a different horizon to aim for...

Refining Life Every Day

Constantly push back the boundaries of what we are capable of. Improving ourselves each day in however small a way, refining how we function within our living and working environment is a magnificent way to live. These tiny adjustments every day are outstandingly self-motivating and will send your self-esteem skyrocketing once the results begin to show for you.

As one who has spent years daily looking at how I might do things better, I can tell you not only does this add to our success mindset, but it also always ensures we constantly feel inspired to achieve more.

Even if you ever feel anxious about something you are contemplating doing for the first time, go ahead anyway and jump right in, then learn as you go along. None of us are born experts, this only comes through experience!

Doesn't matter what this is; however trivial or random it might seem to others or even to us, every single time a small but well-entrenched discomfort zone is overcome it further validates the fact those bigger ones can surely also be taken-on and left in the past...right where they belong.

A significant part of living life as it is meant to be is this willingness to push on regardless of any fear which might well-up inside us, those inner conversations of doubt trying to persuade us to make another poor excuse to stay-put. Carrying right on through without becoming paralysed with procrastination or talking ourselves out of the action.

Rather than being a spectator, choosing to be an active participator in life. Jumping out of that old discomfort zone to confront the mirage of a limitation head on. The compelling sense of inner satisfaction is incomparable. And go through the process once, next time around it is going to be palpably easier. Start small and break down that first comfort trap, then move right on to another.

The only way we can grow is to feel that fear and then take control of over the overwhelming sense of wishing to be someplace else. And then do ourselves the greatest service possible by going right ahead with whatever has always freaked us out to finally do it!

Questions We Ask Ourselves Matter!

The results we achieve long-term depends a lot on the quality of the questions we ask ourselves when events do not go quite according to plan or when presented with challenges in life. Our goals need to stretch us to ask more of ourselves or else we stay-put exactly where we are.

If our inner question are along the lines of "why do these things always happen to me?" or "can I really be bothered with all this stuff?" and "I feel like having a lazy day today, how about I get up at noon?" do you imagine we are placing ourselves in a resourceful mindset?

If we genuinely want to transform our lives, we had better start asking ourselves more empowering questions. "What can I learn from this situation?" or "what can I do differently to achieve all I deserve?" and "I will do whatever I need to make my goals happen for me, however long it takes!".

We Are In Control Of Our Expectations From Others

Bill Bolton's reputation preceded him. Coming across his company through the wholesale business I ran for over a decade, in the trade Bill had unfortunately attracted the generally accepted reputation for being grumpy, cantankerous and abrasive in his way of dealing not only with customers but his own staff!

Yet I knew Bill and I might have a mutually beneficial business relationship. Having talked to him on the phone, I also sensed perhaps Bill chose to be so un-user friendly as a kind of armour, a defence mechanism against the world.

Making an appointment to visit his premises I decided, as I parked my car, I would treat Bill like he was the most friendly and pleasant man I had ever been fortunate enough to meet. For the next hour I reacted like I hadn't noticed his scowl or sour demeanour. Instead I smiled and behaved like he had brightened my day purely for being in his company. Eventually he simply had to start reacting himself more in harmony with the open friendly way he found himself subjected to. To the shock of his staff Bill even laughed at a joke he made himself at one point!

I bought a few items from him, securing a good discount without needing to haggle. Over the next few years I would visit his warehouse once a month. Bill made a point of dealing with me personally and I believe we did become as close to friends as I think he found it possible to allow himself to be. He would drop me an email if he thought he had found an item that would be in my area of interest.

My expectation did indeed bring us mutual success. Rather than believing his reputation, instead I chose to treat Bill as a fellow human I was delighted to meet; and I think to his initial surprise, he found himself reacting in kind to me.

Lives We Deserve

The guy wins big on the lottery and a few years down the line he is right back to square one, having quite effectively managed to squander and lose all his new-found wealth. This windfall found him completely unprepared inside, lacking any internal references for a success orientated mindset he could never feel comfortable living within the reality of being a financially rich person. His mindset being still fixed firmly exactly where it existed prior to his newfound fortune. His entrenched internal programming being one of limited options financially, inevitably leading him straight back into his comfort zone.

Let me share a quick story, you will understand why in a moment...

We had a family cat when I was growing-up, Fluffy she was called (because she really was very Fluffy). When not much more than a year old she hurt a front paw and for a few days limped. There she sat holding her painful paw off the ground. I cannot begin to describe how cute she looked with one paw raised like that and such a sad look on her face. Oh, and did she ever get sympathy – treats and cuddles came her way all day long. Fluffy thankfully recovered from her poorly paw within a week or so. However, for the rest of her happy eighteen years, whenever she wanted a little extra attention or a treat, she would raise one paw off the ground and look sad. And what's more it worked every single time! Clever kitty.

Yet not so clever a mindset for us to adopt if we would prefer health and prosperity.

Sadly illness does also become the comfort zone of some unfortunate people. Perhaps they subconsciously enjoyed all the extra attention coming their way when they were once unwell. We are what we focus on...we get the life we deserve every time.

How many times have you come across someone who, when politely asking how they are, then proceed to solemnly tell you every single detail of every single ailment they are convinced they are burdened with?

Focussing on every possible avenue to wellbeing ensured my own recovery from a rather inconvenient health issue a few years ago. I constantly pushed back the boundaries on what I might achieve by adopting different mindsets or refining my diet. In fact I remain convinced this personally challenging event only happened so I could learn from it to help others!

Learning Opportunities (Aka Mistakes)

All our decisions produce outcomes. These either move us forward immediately if the result is exactly as anticipated or when they do not exactly play-out as we desired, instead they help us move forward a little later. Either way we win!

Mistakes are valuable signposts, feedback from any choices we make which do not immediately produce our desired result. Rather usefully showing us the correct direction to go instead. Every mistake we make is eliminating yet another possible pitfall to increase our chances of reaching our goals.

Wear a mistake on our sleeves we are judging ourselves. Limiting ourselves. Playing the negative feeling into our future, and why would we ever want such thoughts leading to nought? Got to move on, let them go and chose to appreciate the wisdoms gained. Be grateful because here is now another priceless way to avoid making similar errors in the future.

We need to develop the habit of embracing our mistakes, valuing this unique opportunity for feedback. By owning them their power to limit us in any way is gone.

Knowing exactly how NOT to do something is often the greatest gifts of feedback we can get, teaching us far more about the path to our goals than all the success stories in the world could ever do. We certainly all need to value them, avoid negatively dwelling on them and be grateful for the naked truths they show us!

Clearing Up

If our less desirable outcome created a mess we need to clean up after ourselves before being able to fully move on. Point of fact this could well have even been the lesson we needed to learn from the poor choice we made. To take responsibility for the situation, our own life and resolve the consequences arising from our action immediately.

Communicating to build trust again is vital. People will usually forgive mistakes, but never being kept in the dark.

Take direct action and communicate your intentions to those who need to know, everyone respects the person who is visibly taking steps to resolve an issue they created and clean up after themselves.

The whole event is an opportunity for you to shine under duress and brilliantly show the world that this temporary goofing-up moment is never going to define you. You are a person of integrity who stands tall, takes complete responsibility for your actions, and moves on...

Thoughts Leading To Nought

We all inevitably encounter those temporary moments in life where we maybe feel a little sorry for ourselves or ponder why the world is apparently not always seemingly quite so fair. There are some things that come along in life we do struggle to see the upside from.

Many years ago I labelled these moments Thoughts Leading To Nought (aka stinkin' thinkin' as they have also been poetically labelled by some of my fellow coaches). Feeling this way from time to time is part and parcel of our existence as humans. We all experience them and rather usefully we can practically choose to transform away from this rather unhelpful mindset on to something more constructive.

We should never pretend we aren't having Thoughts Leading To Nought; they obviously feel extremely valid at the time. They are also usually there to show us some hitherto unknown truths about our current mindset or possible better choices we can make for ourselves.

Attempting to block out Thoughts Leading To Nought with positive affirmations, without examining exactly why we feel this way, will only ensure the next time a similar event or trigger occurs we are going to feel exactly the same way again only this time more intensely. We need to analyse precisely why we are feeling these emotions before we can move on.

Accept that currently you do feel a little sorry for yourself and that is okay. Own the feeling. So, what can you do about it?

Take two pieces of A4 sized paper, lay them next to one another on a table or another flat surface. On the left-hand piece of paper write down to reveal what specifically about the situation makes you feel the way you do? In terms of perhaps the failure of some well-laid plans or even disappointment with yourself or another. Continue until you have written down everything about the situation that makes you feel the way you do and struggle to move on.

On the right-hand piece of paper write down if there is anything at all you can learn about yourself from the fact you currently feel this bad? Is there something in your lifestyle or decision making which is sitting uncomfortably with you? If this is the case, underneath write down step by step ways you can transform the feelings by making new choices as soon as possible. You now possess that most motivating of gifts to yourself, a set of goals!

When you are done, and you will know when you are, dispose of the first piece of paper. Keep the other one with your new goals. Then take some immediate action to adopt new plans or opt for different lifestyle choices. Sometimes these transformations can be instant, other times they take a while to fully realise and show up in life, however, simply the fact you are actually now taking action will stop Thoughts Leading To Nought right there in their tracks.

Or Is It Simpler Than That?

Or is just one of those bleurgh days we all experience occasionally? Those days when we feel overwhelmed and wonder why life cannot be a little bit simpler?

Here we need to accept that is how we feel right now, it is only temporarily, and everything is really okay long-term.

Re-focussing our energy is simply a matter of recalling a recent happy event we enjoyed and taking a few moments out remembering to feel a little gratitude for all the good experiences we have in life.

And smile! Create some serotonin! Stand up tall and look up!!!

Next time you are having Thoughts Leading To Nought don't beat yourself up over them or feel disappointed with yourself. Accept this is happening and choose to own the moment.

Is there something vital to learn from the experience or is it simply just one of those days? Either way all is okay because occasional Thoughts Leading To Nought are ultimately only part and parcel of having a human experience on this planet.

If you get turned down for the university of your choice, you were never there in the first place, therefore you have lost nothing. You are still in precisely the same position as before you applied. Nothing changed. Go ahead and keep on applying to other universities, eventually one of them will be exactly the right one for you.

Similarly, if the woman/man of your dreams turns down your offer of a date, you were not going out with them before asking. And you are still not going out with them and so again nothing really changed.

What Matters Most? Only You Can Decide...

Neuroscience confirms we are all products of the thoughts we have. Our predominant thoughts permeate through every cell of our brain and body creating the person we are. What we intensely focus on with passion creates powerful energy and scientists can physically measure this energy transmitted by our brains.

There exists a myriad of visual and aural displacements. Many people do choose to prioritise time spent in these trivial displacements rather than authentically living. Each of these displacements ultimately drags us further away from fulfilling our potential. Reaching our goals.

Any time we spend locked-into one or more of these displacements results in us passively falling into inaction. And we stop all the good stuff we would love to welcome into our lives from ever manifesting for us, because our attention is too busy elsewhere on trivia!

There are six major displacements. There are countless other minor ones, but for our purposes here we will talk about the six major ones that impact so dramatically upon so many lives!

Yet there is a flip side here, we have a choice to gain knowledge rather than lock-into displacements. We all have easy access to either knowledge or a displacement anytime we choose. All the time we spend absorbed in any one of these displacements ensures we opt to be passive passengers through life rather than being the captain of our own destiny...

Displacement Number One - Reading Choices

The guy wakes up and before he even gets properly out there into his day he eats his breakfast while working his way through his choice of daily newspaper (or news vlog) reading all about who is killing who, which z-list celebrities have fallen from grace this week and how we are all collectively heading straight into another global recession. Our guy then walks out of his front door with all this stuff running through his head. Not exactly the personally empowered way to begin his day...

What we choose to read powerfully shapes the way we perceive the world. Whichever form our reading literature takes will add to our expectations from life and influence our thinking.

Children act out the characters from their books or comics, adults are the same. As a youth I read spy novels and for sure they influenced my thoughts and behaviour at the time – if I saw a man wearing a tuxedo he was obviously a spy with a hundred concealed gadgets about his person and if someone had a generic Eastern European accent they were clearly intent upon global domination. Ironically I eventually fell in love with Mimi as my life partner, an Eastern European woman (although she seems content with being an English teacher, rather than attempting to be president of the world!).

Reading personally inspiring literature daily helps keep us on-track to our goals.

For over thirty years I have put aside some time for reading every day. If serious about personal growth I am convinced this is essential. Even looking across the room in my creative space at my personal library of all the books I have already absorbed inspires me, happy that knowledge is within me to call upon whenever required.

Our personal library is one of our greatest assets we possess, more valuable to our future than the smartest smartphone.

Reading though not only adds to the breadth of our knowledge, more crucially reading books we find personally inspirational, listening to audios or watching vids/vlogs on a day-to-day basis helps keep our actions centred on our own self-set goals. Consciously keeping us aware of just how important all this is to us.

It is all too easy to get distracted and for the mundane to take centre stage once more in our lives, studying by reading or listening to audios each day is the perfect anchor to constantly re-adjust our radar and keep our inner mojo working.

I am not going to recommend specific authors to inspire you. I believe we all need to follow our own intuition when choosing those books which are going to inspire to us. Personally I find any books, vids or audios by Jim Rohn are timeless, find your own equally inspiring mentors to read. There are many more thousands of choices of self-realisation, wellbeing, and autobiographical inspirational books out there. Check them out at libraries or bookstores and you will immediately know which ones speak to you.

Displacement Number Two - Television

What we view on television is not called a programme for nothing. Everything we watch on television is passively programming us with usually fictional dialogue and images created by other people we do not personally know. By the way, rather alarmingly our brain does not necessarily register this experience as fictional and treats the input essentially the same as any real-life experiences!

The programmes we watch, the characters we habitually welcome into our life via television become our crowd. Just like in real life, those main people we hang-out with we either come up or down to the same level as. Rule of thumb here is would we personally wish be friends with those characters we welcome directly into our heads via television or engage in living exactly their kind of life? No? Then quickly choose to tune into another channel or turn it off.

> Just 4 hours spent each day watching television over a week = **28 hours**
>
> So 28 hours every week over a whole month of watching television = **5 whole days**
>
> Then 5 whole days a month watching television across an entire year = **2 months' worth of lost days**

Imagine how amazing it would be if you were offered gratis a whole sixty extra days this year? How much further forward towards fulfilling your own dreams would you be right now if gifted those whole two free extra months to pursue your goals?

Displacement Number Three – The Internet

The internet obviously has the potential to be wonderfully informative and enlightening. There are some amazing people out there the internet affords us often direct contact with. My own personal network around the world includes incredible pioneering individuals, fellow free-thinkers one and all. Through communicating globally we ensure we are all collectively raising awareness of the same principles. Those eternal codes for constructing a life of our own making. Those very same codes which have proved their effectiveness through the validation of amazing results time and time again, right down through the centuries. I am one voice, thankfully there are many more and personally I feel constantly grateful for the platform afforded by the internet which has allowed me and my message to become globally known.

At the other end of the scale, a well-known car magazine recently conducted their own independent survey of the videos posted online showing any budding amateur mechanic viewers how to fix the braking system of a popular make of car. They were horrified to discover nearly 50% of the videos were either incomplete or erroneous in some way and around 10% of the advice offered, if followed, would prove lethal! As they commented in their editorial "anyone with a camera can post a vid offering words of wisdom about fixing brakes, without any bona fide experience or mechanical knowledge and there is not a thing anyone can do about it". Imagine the consequences should similar health advice be followed...

Practically anyone can post anything to the internet. Right now I could start posting videos offering my uninformed opinions on thermo-dynamics or perhaps even more catastrophic for my viewers, run a blog giving out fashion advice!

All too often many of us tend to unconditionally believe what we see or read on the internet, trusting that what we are reading or watching must be established fact beyond ever questioning its validity or the motivation existing behind the message.

Whilst there are some amazing websites and vlogs out there, informing and entertaining; there are also some ludicrously ignorant and seriously ill-informed people posting stuff online. Then there are those who find it amusing to intentionally mis-inform viewers or possess a nefarious desire to negatively mass manipulate others. Well publicised court cases recently confirming how frighteningly easy it turned out to be for those sad individuals to unfortunately make others take actions way outside of their own best interests.

Vloggers are fertile hunting ground for companies wanting some useful product placement, especially if the vlogger they target has enough followers. If our favourite vlogger talks up a make-up line, fashion brand, car, computer game, food/drink or indeed more or less any other consumer item, chances are they will be getting paid fees in exchange for the exposure. Successful vloggers do reach many millions of followers every time they post a vid, what a responsibility! Let's hope they don't have any hidden agendas as they are so well respected by our youth for their opinions...

Displacement Number Four – Music Choices

Music creates feelings and feelings create our reality. The energy music gives off directly affects the cells of our body and minds. This one has been scientifically proven beyond any possible doubt. Famous experiments conclusively showing how various types of music directly affects the wellbeing of plants and water molecules in a positive or negative way. Imagine then how music choices will also be affecting the more sophisticated form of life known as you?

Many of us download music directly into our heads through noise-cancelling headphones. If your pleasure involves listening to music which actually has pretty poor or unevolved messages in the lyrics, sorry to have to be the one to inform you, but you are dramatically self-limiting your personal potential by directly programming your subconscious with trash!

I am not suggesting you need to now go and delete or sell your entire catalogue of music if you are into thrash-metal, emo bands or whatever; but you will definitely do yourself a great favour if you buy-out of listening to for at least a week and then see if you feel any different.

Inspirational contemporary music or from the amazing back-catalogue of classical composers created with metaphysical awareness, motivates us rather than keeping us down. As with books, I am avoiding suggesting specific musical choices here, we need to trust our intuition and anyway we all have our own preferences for genres of music. And furthermore, I am convinced that we do really always truthfully know what is best for ourselves, even if sometimes we tend to ignore our gut instinct. I ignored mine for years with my own choice of music...

I would drive along in my car singing away to certain long-term favourite bands and what's more I already knew how self-limiting some of their lyrics were! Eventually, through the course of writing this book, I finally went through my entire music collection in a more discerning way, discarding all the negative stuff I did not want to programme my subconscious mind with. I had been aware of the power of music to influence our mindsets for well over three decades; walking our talk takes as long as it takes!

Displacement Number Five - Gaming

Computer games, such as those with brightly coloured quickly moving images designed to keep us playing on, are also stopping us from doing things to positively take charge of our life. You know the score, we are talking here about the ones widely marketed via television and pop-ups or sidebar adverts on websites, enticing us all to join in the fun to carry right on addictively playing to reach infinitely ever higher levels.

A few years ago a friend asked me to child-mind her seven-year-old boy for an hour as she had some errands to run in the city and they would be easier to accomplish if temporarily child free. Sitting with this boy I asked him what he wanted to do and he told me he was unhappy he did not have his mum's laptop because what he really wanted to do was play his favourite computer game. I suggested instead we build something with the well-known brand of various coloured plastic interlocking bricks and begrudgingly he agreed.

Getting out the bricks and making a start, all the way through our construction he constantly mimicking the noises of a computer game. And I mean remarkably realistic imitations of people being shot, explosions and from time to time he would proclaim himself dead.

Attempting to engage him in normal conversation was a challenge as he replied in video game speak and wanted me to join in with his acting out role-playing the different characters from his favourite game. I sensed he must have wondered which planet I had beamed-in from when it became clear to him I had no idea what he was talking about. That was one exceptionally long hour as I waited for his mum to return. And it did disturb me more than a little the level at which he partly existed all the time within this well-known game.

When I have been to parent evenings for my stepdaughter, often the subject of computer games does come up. She shows little interest in them. Her teachers have all said year after year as she progresses through school, without exception, they can always tell the children in class who spend a lot of time playing computer games, in terms of their attention span, their communication skills and the level to which they are able to interactively participate with their peers in class.

Displacement Number Six - Smartphones

Imagine creating this device which could pacify massive swathes of the population, those who live in most technologically developed countries.

These people would voluntarily spend most of their time investing their main attention on this device to the detriment of observing the reality of genuine life going on around them. Regardless of this being direct interaction with fellow humans, changes in their rights as citizens, enjoying nature, life going on in the city or indeed that truck heading right for them as they blithely stand right there in middle of the street absorbed in their screen.

Better still how about we get the user's fingerprints/ scans of their faces/eyes as part of the process and gather all of their personal details - like who they communicate with and every email they send; who they bank with and how they spend their money down to the last penny or cent; where they are geographically located to within a metre at any given time, their interests and social media posts; if they are away on vacation and where they went; where they work or not; who they hang-out with and where they hang-out with them; what they had for lunch or even what time they usually go to bed and who with; then is all starts again when they get up the following day to eat breakfast!

And how about as part of this process we make this device so addictive to the users they consider it essential to their very survival, a vital part of their identity and day to day functioning. Their life.

Even better still let's make the users pay out their own pockets for the privilege of being indoctrinated. Talk about a masterplan!

You really couldn't make it up...

At my talks and workshops I can virtually guarantee at some point, as I actively encourage audience interaction and a two-way dialogue, someone is going to bring up the subject of smartphones. This discussion will generally proceed along the lines of many audience members denouncing smartphones as being intrusive, time stealing and over-priced, some even going so far as to confirm they feel these devices control lives. You get the picture, the majority of those who contribute to these group discussions will have an inherent distaste for this piece of technology.

After we have all talked for a little while I ask my audience to raise their hands if they have a smartphone upon their person.

You guessed, almost 100% of audience members will put their hand up!

Then usually follows laughter. Naturally, I ask why. Their answers reveal they fear that if they don't use their smartphone they will be missing out on what their friends are up to and consider themselves to be out of the loop.

I personally don't own a smartphone. I haven't used one for over ten years now. I do possess a phone; it has just got a seriously low technological IQ. I can make or receive calls, which is about all I require it to do.

I usually bring out my own phone to show everyone at these seminars, when the inevitable subject rears its head, and there is collective amazement that a writer, broadcaster and public speaker can function with such a dim-light of a phone here in the 21st century.

I am happy to share a collective laugh at the expense of my little phone, yet I also hope it might open a few eyes. I show options, it's for others to decide what truly matters to them.

There are now clinics existing in most developed countries to treat teenager's and the even younger, for their addiction to smartphones. Ongoing studies by universities across the world are universally confirming that using a smartphone directly affects the user's brain.

Think about your still-developing child's brain, is even the slightest possibility of any potential harmful side-effects from long-term smartphone exposure worth the risk?

It is clearly sensible and logical for minors when out and about to be able to keep in contact with their parents and vice versa, to also communicate with their peers. How about restricting the use of smartphones to those under sixteen years old? Those younger than sixteen can still have phones capable of making calls and sending texts, but with safely mega-low electro-magnetic emissions and no direct access to surf the internet.

When we are a teenager or even in our twenties living on our phone may well seem like a perfectly legitimate use of our time...how about in our forties or fifties?

Will we be happy at fifty years old to look back and reflect upon the lost years we spent absorbed in our phones rather than building an amazing life to enjoy when we are that much further down our timeline?

I am not suggesting for one moment it is too late at fifty or even later to turn our life around. Many wonderful examples confirm that we can build an exciting new future at any point in our lives. Only would it not have been rather cooler to have already given ourselves a brilliant head start by climbing on to our personal ladder of success three decades earlier to now be reaping the rewards?

A Personal Empowerment Experiment

It is all down to what we want from life. That word choice again.

The more we do anything the more engrained it becomes within our neural pathways. Yet even with the most powerfully habitual of our actions, if we stop doing them for even a short period of time, the neural pathway becomes less predominant and predeterminate to our actions.

If we can replace any self-displacements with something more constructive the chances of falling back into those old patterns of behaviour are dramatically reduced.

If you know for sure that you personally buy into any of those six major self-defeating displacements I ask you to allow yourself to indulge in a little experiment...I would like you to spend three whole days without buying into your personal choice of distraction/s. Go completely cold turkey.

"Excuse me?!"

"You're asking me to do what here?!!!"

I hear what you are saying and feel your shock. Please stay with me here, you have practically nothing to lose and might well gain something life transforming. All I ask for is only those three days commitment to this experiment out of your hopefully long life, so why not just give this one a go? You can always go back to how you did things before once these three days are up, now a little better informed about yourself. And self-learning is never wasted.

If you take hours devouring every word of a daily newspaper or news vlog, avoid doing this during these three days. Leave the TV turned off if that is your thing. Check emails then avoid surfing the internet if you usually spend practically every waking hour engaged on it. If your pleasure involves listening to music which actually has negative messages in the lyrics (and don't pretend you don't know exactly the type I am talking about here!) buy-out of listening during your experiment. Play no computer games if they usually take your attention. And finally use your phone only for essential communication if it is usually your life.

- DAY ONE - Okay, here we go! This first day is going to feel extremely unsettling and disturbing as you take on a radically different daily routine. Keep yourself busy doing something else, can be anything at all which distracts you from your usual distraction! Clean out a closet, have a walk, take a pen and paper to sketch something, write a poem, talk with family or friends, visit someplace you haven't been before; anything at all to occupy yourself with a positive action so you feel you are gaining from the experience.

- DAY TWO - Hanging on in there. This second day will more than likely see you constantly craving the missing element from your life. As with yesterday, be sure to keep yourself occupied and stick with the experiment anyway, after all only one more day to go...

- DAY THREE - Life feels different. You have held in there for two days already, how about now taking a look around at what you might do long-term that you do not normally have the time for? What action can you take right now to commence making a few more long-term positive changes in your life? If you have not yet got a library of enlightening or motivating books or audios, check out to see what is available. If your goals require new qualifications or skill sets have a look at what college courses exist locally or online and visit or email them to make a firm commitment. Connect to some interesting local contacts or even learn to meditate.

To make any changes stick we crucially need to replace our old paradigm with a massively more engaging new one we can enjoy living.

Friendship And Other Company We Keep

I always did my best to get an appointment anywhere far away then I could avoid attending the office end of year party and unfortunately never seemed to quite manage to pull this one off. This was in my old corporate days working in commercial publishing and as head of a department attending this big annual social event was an obligation (but not if I wasn't there!).

To be honest I found one or two of my office-based colleagues bleakly challenging to spend too much time around. During the year I would typically be out there on the road attending meetings and delivering pitches averagely three or four days a week. Attending this party rather inconveniently brought me into all too close proximity with those very people I nicely managed to avoid for the rest of the year quite effectively.

This was back before smoking inside of restaurants became banned by law. This event would see me spending several gruellingly long hours listening to expletively ridden moaning about how bad life at the office was or else drunken ego tripping, all while as I attempted to peer out of watering eyes through a thick fog of cigarette smoke to make out who I was reluctantly talking with anyway. All in all one thoroughly grim experience. Ouch!

I have ensured during the decades since of running several of my own businesses to surround myself with people who buy-into why we do what we do and feel part of a happy team. And equally importantly we all collectively ensure our work environment is consistently a fun place to be – and definitely never a compulsory to attend end of year party!

The Upside

We have all met those fabulous gems of people who make us feel great about life just by being in their presence. Then there are those friends who, no matter how long since we last enjoyed their company, spending time together again things slot straight back into the friendship, conversation easily flowing like you have never been apart.

For sure though not everyone we encounter has quite this harmonious an effect. There are also those unfortunate people who are rather more challenging to be around.

Although widely known these days (yet not always taken anything like seriously enough) the main five people we spend the most time with are those we end up coming to the same level as socially, emotionally, and economically. Clearly then our crowd can either help us or hinder us, it all depends.

Greetings And Adios To The Dream-Stealers

We have all met the type. Those prophets of doom who can only see the negative in everyone and everything they encounter. Those who can make the brightest sunny day seem damp and cold only for spending some time in their doom-ridden company. These dream-stealing people love nothing better than to rain on our parade. And although they seldom seem to ever achieve a great deal in their own lives, they do nevertheless consider themselves perfectly qualified to judge us, advise us, and attempt to quell our enthusiasm for where we are going in our own life.

As you and I tend to see the bigger picture we know these people have ongoing issues playing forward into their life, seeing others making progress sadly compels them to do their level best to bring everyone else down on to their level of reality then they don't feel quite so dis-empowered. Everyone has the right evolve at their own pace, dream-stealers are no different, for sure though this never means to say we are required to also buy into their mindset!

Taking it as established fact that we really do wish to evolve into our full potential, as discerning individuals we need to take care to have an impartial look around our own immediate circle. And then choose to stay far away from any of those dream-stealing stress-inducing acquaintances who make it feel like an hour spent in their company lasts like a wet fortnight...

For the sake of your own long-term wellbeing and economic future avoid hanging-out with dream-stealers at all costs!

Higher Friends

As we are going to end up coming to the same level as our crowd, how about seeking out potential friends with greater knowledge or those possessing brightly shining positively minded attitudes to life?

Having these friends engenders within us the often much appreciated aspiration and motivation to become the best version of ourselves as well.

Spending down-time with our evolved circle of friends can contrastingly show us many truths about ourselves and help us to stretch our potential for greatness. Brilliant friends are those who never judge, seeking as they do the same things from life as we do, motivated by the desire to further evolve and be happier.

Negative People Are There To Teach Us

How true, and those challenging people who enter in our lives all have something we can learn from and how often it is all about ourselves. Wonderfully poetic if you think about it, after all how else can it possibly be if we are to grow beyond being a victim of circumstance and reclaim back the power to control our own destiny?

If the people we are surrounding ourselves with are negative thinkers, it is going to have a knock-on effect to our own mindset. We might think it will not affect us, but negative thinkers will always have a drip drip drip effect on our mindset regardless of us being consciously aware of it.

We need to raise our standards. Raise our standards about who we choose to spend our time with and give our attention to.

So how about those extreme examples of horribly behaving individuals we all occasionally encounter? Are we meant to tolerate their company regardless of their frequently shocking words or actions?

The lessons the particularly obnoxious behaviour of others can teach us is their actions are unacceptable, and that we deserve better. We need to raise our standards. It is our right (and indeed their path) to disassociate from such people.

Some people still have bigger lessons to learn about themselves. Whilst their nasty behaviour is showing forth their need to address their own issues and deal with them this certainly never compels us to become a part of the daily chaos of their life or ever put up with disrespectful treatment.

The opinion of these self-defeating highly negative people is seldom what is seems. Any hurtful vitriol (which is extreme poor thinking vocalized) directed towards us is of practically no importance whatsoever. Unless we allow it to be. Buying into their viewpoint by validating ourselves or defending our position, gives their opinion the power to control the way we feel. Their mindset is informed by their own experiences, we are just a handy target by being in their vicinity.

Assuming you do not agree with the negative statements made about you to your face (and these sentiments really are never personal or valid to who you are) simply let them go, treating their opinions as totally irrelevant. Your reality is different, and now it is time to move on in peace. Let them have the freedom to evolve at their own pace or not. As is their choice.

If we do occasionally need to come into contact with people with this negative kind of programme running through their actions and we just let it all wash over us, then walk away when we can do, our stress levels will drop dramatically!

Addicted To Drama

Before we finish talking about challenging people, we also need to remain vigilant that some of those we encounter are addicted to drama in their lives. Through this understanding, whenever we encounter such toxic behaviour, we can view their reactions and mindset more within context.

Drama addicts are going through life running an internal programme pre-set to chaotic situations. And if life is not giving them enough of their default setting, unfortunately they create drama for themselves and all those around them.

Whenever we encounter a drama addict we can bring ourselves much inner peace by choosing to buy-out of any of their toxic behaviour. This person is consistently creating this reality for themselves wherever they may go and more than likely with whoever they are around.

On a subconscious level chaos or confrontation is constantly all the drama addict seeks, even though it clearly makes them unhappy.

Opting to remain calmly detached, rather than giving up our centre by getting too personally involved in their dramas and not reacting if they are more aggressive towards us, will allow us to retain our personal power. Far better for our immediate and long-term wellbeing than being manipulated into trading insults!

After all the drama addict will be carrying this programme with themselves to play forward into any situation or through any person they encounter. We are on the receiving end this time because we are handily right there with them at that moment. Next time it will be someone else.

We must remain alert to the truth that with drama addicts their behaviour is indiscriminate. It is all about them and their own issues, never anything personal relating to us.

We cannot teach anyone knowledge they are not yet ready to learn. There is little point in saying too much to a drama addict about their self-defeating poor thinking mindset, rather better we keep attention on living on our own terms and let them evolve at their own pace.

In every case showing by example works more effectively than verbally attempting to show the drama addict how self-defeating their mindset is, it is the kinder way for them and you...

Meditation - Let's Take A Journey

I would like to share with you my own personal method of meditating because I feel that what I have developed can benefit so many others as well. This has evolved over the course of some thirty years and still continues to expand, providing new forms of enlightenment along the way. All those I have taught this method to have been able to meditate almost straight away and subsequently adapt what they have learned to suit their own needs.

In meditation there is no right or wrong, it is the level of understanding and personal experience or insight that ultimately matters the most. In explaining my own methodology I am merely showing one possible path. There are many others, if my method doesn't speak to you I strongly recommend exploring further until you find one that fits you perfectly.

If meditation happened to be taught in schools there would be an upcoming generation of young people who would be able to solve all of the global issues we are currently facing, together with automatically already possessing an empathy and compassion for their fellow humans.

When I first consciously set out on my spiritual journey of growth in the late 1980's I read hundreds of books, travelled to sacred sites and treated the whole experience as something purely intellectual to be studied and memorized. I could quote those books word for word!

Experience has taught me that the road to evolvement is experiential, requiring dedication and commitment. Sacrifices will have to be made. Yet like in all good things in life, those sacrifices are often willingly made in order for the greater understanding that ultimately results as the end manifestation. An example would be in terms of a lot of popular culture and by this I mean most television programmes and a fairly large proportion of commercial radio-friendly music which jars quite significantly with my desire to reach the highest level of well-being and be the best version of myself possible. We will go further into this in the next chapter We Need To Talk, when we explore ways in which the power of words transforms how we experience life.

Negativity of others no longer affects me in the way it once did. Other than to feel a deep sense of compassion,

sending love and, and through experience I am at least able to see where their behaviour and reactions more than likely originate from.

How did I reach this state of compassionate, love and active detachment? Through meditation, the absolute peace of mind and inner serenity that most of us who choose to meditate feel.

The Journey Inside And Outside

Firstly, I would like you to meet yourself!

If you have never meditated before I can tell you that this is quite an eye-opening experience. In actuality this is a something of a dramatic understatement, it is not only eye-opening, but also positively astounding!

If we wish to grow to any significant degree we are logically going to have to know and understand ourselves as completely as possible. If we are sincere in our desire to heal past events moving forward in love and freedom, what is needed is a fast-track method of reaching our subconscious mind or inner self.

It goes without saying that you are going to need to find somewhere quiet, a place that there is no chance you are likely to be disturbed. Later, as you will no doubt discover, it is possible to meditate pretty much anywhere (trains are a favourite place of mine, the rhythm and movement of the train is a wonderful assistance for deeply relaxing) for now though finding a quiet location is essential.

You may have seen films or as in the picture on page 134, the classic meditation position, sitting on a cushion, comfortably cross-legged and with the back straight? If crossing your legs feels uncomfortable, sit in an upright chair instead and again, have your back straight.

Breathe steadily. In and out. Becoming aware of only your own breathing.

As you relax and feel the tension leaving your body. You are going on a journey. An inward journey to the very centre of the you of you.

Picture in your mind an elevator door. This is your very own magical travel capsule. Now see the door opening and you are stepping inside. The door closes behind you. You feel very safe cocooned in your magical elevator.

You look at the numbers illuminated above the door and see that you are currently at level 0. The lift starts to move slowly downward and you see -1 appear, then -2 as you continue down.

Becoming more relaxed with every number that passes.

With each number as you descend you are getting closer to the real you of you. -3...-4...-5.

Now leaving the everyday world far behind as you continue through -6 and -7. Deeper and deeper. -8 and -9.

Finally level -10 is reached.

Slowly the door slides open and you venture out of your internal elevator. Time has no meaning here. You are right in the heart of your own subconscious. Moving with caution, start to float around and explore.

What can you sense? What can you feel? And see?

At first this is the oddest experience. Stay calm and take your time to absorb the sensations. All of your own experiences and knowledge are right here...to attempt to access all of it in one go would be unrealistic.

Simply float along and passively observe this first time.

When you feel that your journey is done for this meditation make your way back to your internal elevator.

It is right there waiting for you, as it always has been and always will be.

The door opens and you step back inside. The number above the door is still there at level -10.

Watch the numbers as the elevator slowly automatically rises, right through back to level 0 once again, our normal waking state. The door opens. You can now open your eyes.

Congratulations you have finally met yourself!

I do know how you are feeling and it can be pretty, shall we say, mind expanding. Take a little time to allow the experience to sink in fully and then, when you feel ready, take the inward journey again. This time you will be more prepared for what to expect and can explore further. In fact, as you become more adept you can even choose to seek out certain parts of your subconscious to explore and visit...

The Next Step - Make This Actually A Useful Exercise And Gain Personally From It

Please be aware that we all have the absolute ability to edit our subconscious. That is to jettison the unwanted garbage that will have accumulated there. Anything that might be limiting or stopping us from getting where we wish to be is there to be exposed ready to be cleansed.

Personally I find the easiest way to do this is to image anything I wish to reject as a dark cloud and see it being placed neatly into an airlock I have imaged right there in my own subconscious. Now the door of the airlock is closing and the negativity is trapped right in there. There is a large red button positioned next to the airlock door and when I press it the outside door opens and then the negative thought or aspect I wished to cleanse passes out into space to be cast onto the purifying solar winds, never to return. It is done.

Meditation acts not only on the rogue thought or feeling, but it also actually affects our cell memory of the event as well!

Now we know how to travel within, how do we travel outwards from ourselves into different levels of knowing and existence?

This is called journeying and as the song says... The only way out is in!

I teach guided meditation and in essence this is about deciding before starting out on our inner journey what it is we wish to experience or where we wish to travel. Once the decision is made, keep the suggestion in your mind as you travel in your magical elevator and once you reach the centre of your being...push outwards.

Use your own subconscious mind as only the starting point and springboard to explore outside of yourself. It is safe to do this. If at any point you feel uncomfortable or like you wish to return, all you have to do is think the thought and there you will be right back in your subconscious before your internal elevator door.

I am often asked what is possible by practising meditation and further via journeying during meditating. At the very least a deeper sense of self will be achieved, plus regular meditation has been proved to aid concentration and majorly de-stress. Possibilities within journeying are pretty much limited only by our own perception of possibility!

Another question I get asked is how real journeying experiences are. "Well that all depends!" is the slightly cryptic answer I usually give. There are some great master meditators who journey to actual physical locations in the World, subsequently being able to describe these places in intricate and accurate detail. Equally so there are those who feel sure they are reaching higher levels of existence during their meditations, even sometimes interacting with others during this experience; of course, by its very nature this is impossible to prove or disprove, however, that hardly makes the wisdoms and insights gained any less valid.

My advice is if it feels right and your gut tells you so...99% of the time it is going to be right! I believe that we all inherently know deep down, and this applies in any sphere of life as well as meditation, if what we are doing or are about to do is right for us. Meditation teaches us more about ourselves and can definitely assist in learning to trust our own instinct and going with what feels right.

Yet There Is More

I left the decision on if I should include or exclude this final section right up until I reached this point. Further to what we just talked about, my intuition is telling me that I do need to include it for those who are ready now to take this step or for others to give them hope for the day when the allotted moment arrives when they can also undertake this journey.

We all have that part of us that is outside of the physical body. Some call this higher self, soul, spirit. Whatever label we care to place upon on, for ease of description and because this is how I personally perceive it, I am going to refer to it here as our higher self.

It is possible to contact our own higher self through meditation. There is a doorway, it exists for all who have the courage to seek it and this doorway is accessed through our subconscious mind. Seek it out during the deepest meditation and eventually you will find it.

Unless you are an ascended master living on Earth who is currently unaware of this fact, you will find that the door to your higher self is closed.

Can this door be opened, the gateway to our own divine essence? Yes, it can.

You need to remain aware that to glimpse the divine is never to be taken lightly.

I am not going to tell you how the door looks. It shows itself differently for each individual. Seek it though and if you are ready, you will find it. And you will definitely know when you have!

Exercise extreme caution when attempting this. I have opened my own personal door more than once. I am going to leave it for you to discover for yourself what the experience feels like, other than to say it is like nothing on Earth! Cleansing and healing in a way that is indescribable in words. It needs to be experienced to fully understand.

I chose to share this with you as I honestly believe that humanity is reaching a point of evolution where all those who are ready need to know this information. Those who are not, well they will be unable to open the door, even if they do manage to find it, which is less than likely.

Paradoxically, at times the door to our higher self will be opened from the other side, without our even being aware of it. By our own higher self communicating with us. Those moments of pure inspiration we sometimes experience or those ideas that are so completely perfect, those come from our own higher self.

Cultivate the habit of making friends with your higher self and sincerely attempt to reach it through meditation and those inspirational moments will happen more often.

Enjoy meditation on whatever level feels right for you. Journeying will happen for you when you are ready and all the enlightenment you need personally to grow will manifest perfectly at the allotted moment for you.

We Need To Talk

Words are like the gears that put any of our emotions or feelings into action in our lives.

Others you engage in conversation hear only a fraction of the entire catalogue of words you speak each day. You hear them all, every single word. You are the constant secret eavesdropper on all your private conversations, even those you have with yourself!

The Power Within Words

This powerful truth bears repeating - whatever we focus on with great intensity, those thought patterns we give our attention to much of the time; makes us who we are. We are constantly creating or manifesting the life we live, yet our thoughts are only partly responsible, as I know by now you are beginning to realise.

Words are the actual catalyst that outwardly expresses our feelings, the emotions relating to our current life situation.

Words Change Everything

By consciously changing our choice of any self-limiting words, those we habitually use when describing our life or an emotional state, we possess a magical tool to completely transform that same life of ours instantly.

I AM = two of the most powerful words in existence, for those two words are always followed by a direct reference to how we feel, our emotional response to a situation or our actual wellbeing.

Whatever is added to those two power words, I AM, unconditionally ensures directly exactly the experiences we have in life. And our happiness, wellbeing, and success (or not!).

We use I AM to create our life when we say:

- *I am usually sad **or** I am typically happy.*
- *I am often ill **or** I am looking for ways to heal quickly.*
- *I am so bored **or** I am fascinated to learn.*
- *I am poor **or** I am successful.*
- *I am feeling old **or** I am as young as I feel.*
- *I am too shy to do new stuff **or** I am confident operating outside comfort zones.*
- *I am weak **or** I am strong.*

- *I am undeserving **or** I am worthy of only good stuff happening in my life, learning opportunities teach me.*
- *I am furious **or** I am slightly irritated.*
- *I am unable to deal with all this **or** I am sure I will cope, there is always a way.*
- *I am utterly devastated **or** I am a little perturbed.*
- *I am deeply upset **or** I am a bit disgruntled.*
- *I am completely overwhelmed **or** I am making an action plan.*
- *I am totally lost **or** I am looking for another way.*
- *I am so full of problems **or** I am dealing with challenges one by one.*

So many times our words end up as disproportionately over-reactions to the events happening around us. For sure challenges come along in life, it happens, how we choose to describe those challenges goes a long way to us either feeling far worse or finding some inner strength to see the light at the end of the tunnel.

If we describe one of those challenging individuals we all encounter from time to time, like a dream-stealer or drama addict, as "completely messing with my head" or "they make me feel sick!" or worse still "I feel like jumping off a bridge after I've been around him for any time!"; we quite efficiently ensure the situation feels many times worse for us than it need be. And why would we choose to do that? For sure though so many of us do choose to buy into precisely that kind of reaction when encountering challenging people or situations.

Every time we make one of those big statements, although we may well sound theatrically dramatic and passionate, all we are effectively doing is adding massively more poor thinking energy into whatever the situation might be and guaranteeing we consequently feel considerably worse than we actually need to.

When we do find ourselves needing to temporarily spend some time around any of those people whose personal energy clashes with our own, why not instead describe the encounter as "slightly challenging" or "a bit irritating" or better still "I am easily able to deal with guys like that, my happiness is down to me!".

How about health issues? If we have a "such a bad headache it feels like my skull is being squeezed" or "now I have a debilitating flu to deal with" perhaps "such bad insomnia, I can barely keep my eyes open" does anyone seriously expect to quickly heal if this is how they describe how they feel?

On the contrary it is going to make any of us feel even less well and ensure that feeling lasts for as long as possible.

How about instead "slight discomfort in my head" a "bit of a cold" perhaps "I will take a quick power nap, then I am sure to feel better".

For some invaluable self-healing techniques see later chapter A Mindful Approach To Health beginning on page 192.

This subject of words is so important I have evolved our very own Personal Freedom Thesaurus, to get us thinking about the words we habitually use. Taking this as purely a starting point, do yourself this greatest service, choose a day to quickly jot down in a notebook any words or phrases you habitually use. Those words central to your typical descriptive vocabulary and which could well be limiting your potential. I did this myself many years ago and found myself shocked with how I described myself and my life! I wish you to have your own similarly eye-opening experience.

Prove this one for yourself by doing the exercise and using our Thesaurus. You have absolutely nothing to lose and stand to gain a lot in terms of the brand-new paradigm for living you will be creating.

Personal Freedom Thesaurus

I'M SO DUMB/STUPID/AN IDIOT - if you are always putting yourself down you have personally also given the world and its' siblings the right to treat you badly.

Vitally important for your immediate wellbeing to permanently delete this habit from your internal programming and vocabulary as this produces such a negative effect upon your direct experience of life.

There is no dumb/stupid/idiot by the way - if you do not know something it is because you have yet to learn it. Does not make you stupid, simply gifts a learning opportunity to discover something new. Avoid at all costs labelling yourself dumb, stupid or an idiot. If you want to know about a subject then go and find out more so you are informed. If it fails to interest you, leave it alone and all is good, so what? There is no rule which says we need to know everything about everything. Expressing opinions on how dumb we are or how awful we look on a day-to-day basis gives permission for everyone else to be critical of us as well!

I HAVE SO MANY PROBLEMS – ouch! This is going to make anything we need to deal with seem big and scary. Some people seem to wear their challenges in life like some kind of badge of honour. We ask them how they are doing and they instantly come back with "oh, I have so many problems!" as they then proceed to list them, usually counting them off on their fingers as they talk. We all have things that come along in life we have not anticipated from time to time, it happens.

A new paradigm is needed if everything unforeseen is viewed in terms of unsurmountable problems. How about re-labelling the issue as A CHALLENGE? A challenge for sure brings out the best in us, guaranteeing we go on dealing with it right through to its satisfactory conclusion. A challenge is always psychologically self-motivational, something to solve and see through.

MY LIFE IS SO BAD – self-pity is incredibly self-limiting. Indulging in feeling sorry for ourselves is self-perpetuating, until we decide to break the pattern. Far better to go ahead to interrupt this limiting mindset by feeling a little gratitude for all the things in life we so often take for granted. Like a roof over our heads, food to eat, friends and family, pets or any of the other thousand and one things we all tend to perhaps take a little bit for granted, yet ought to feel heartfelt gratitude for.

Our happiness is always right there in our hands. How about smiling (serotonin, remember), looking up and proclaiming I AM FEELING GOOD (sounds a bit like the beginning of a cool song) or LIFE IS AWESOME!

ALARM CLOCK – Here is an example of how a small shift in a label made for a radical shift in my own attitude to my day. Every morning for quite a few years my clock went 'brng, brng' and I saw it as an alarm. Now, for me an alarm is something calamitous "Oh no, an alarm!" and it set me leaping out of bed already alarmed and wondering what next alarming thing was going to happen.

Eventually I realised this is silly and I re-labelled it my WAKE-UP CALL. It is still the clock going 'brng, brng' at that part of the day when I get up but labelling it my wake-up call rather than an alarm, well that is motivational "what can I do today?", it is inspirational, "I have had my wake-up call let's go and see what I can do to change the world today!"

Just one small difference in the way we label something, and for sure significant changes in attitude and feelings do happen.

I'LL TRY - trying implies making a half-hearted effort to do something. "I gave it a go, at least I tried".

To try can hardly be considered making a resolutely determined commitment to succeed whatever obstacles may cross our path. In fact, quite the opposite. Try as a word is ultimately rather trying!

Some alternative words rather than try or trying – I WILL DO, I AM COMMITTED TO DOING WHATEVER IT TAKES and I NEED TO DO IT AND I WILL.

IT'S IMPOSSIBLE - if the great thinkers of the past few centuries had subscribed to things being impossible we would not have electricity, xylophones, digital watches, telescopes, surrealist art or any of the million and one other things we usually take for granted. To the closed minds of those times these great inventions or contributions to the arts must have seemed completely impossible. And yet they happened. Brunel, Mozart, Einstein, Mark Twain and Dali (and all the other geniuses) for sure must have met their fair share of dream stealers. Thankfully for the sake of everyone else they ignored them.

Anything Possible is ACHIEVABLE! If something is literally able to happen in any sense at all then it ceases to be impossible. It just takes determination and maybe some lateral thinking for it to manifest. I am not going to suggest alternative words for this one only a beautifully open mind and a reminder of this quote from a famous movie actress and great humanitarian, "nothing is impossible, even the word itself contains I'm Possible!"

I SHOULD - is showing a lack of real commitment. "I should wash those dishes" is not going to get those dishes washed. Should implies that for sure in theory we need to do something, but we are not really going to. Should is a cop-out phrase. I should go to University and get some qualifications is making a statement about a possibility, without any kind of commitment. The absolute best alternative words rather than should are I WILL and even better I AM!

I HATE – oh boy, this one does make me cringe inside when I hear it. I mean I cannot help but actually wince to hear people start a statement with those two words "I hate". And it is so often a seriously disproportionally strong proclamation to make about something or even a person we dislike.

So many atrocities and gross acts against humanity in the past have been done in the name of and justified by those two words "I hate". This phrase sends out an immensely powerful message into the universe about our way of judging situations and people. The hate energy for sure permeates through every cell of our brain and body as well. What we focus on, the energy we put out there into the universe attracts more of the similar energy back to us. When selecting "I hate" as a descriptive statement about anything, we are attracting many more situations or people to also hate into our lives. Would any of us consciously wish to bring more things to hate into the direct experience of our lives? I hope that you will agree with me when I say that I sure know I would not wish to attract anything to hate directly into my life and trust you feel the same!

How about choosing NOT TO MY TASTE as a positively focussed statement? "She is not to my taste as a person" or "That area is not to my taste" etc,.

Of course, if there is someone or something causing any of us to genuinely feel for real such a radically strong reaction as real hate, we need to remove them or it from our life as promptly as we possibly can!

I FEEL SO ILL - is one sure way of ensuring that we are certainly going to feel worse and take longer to recover. Rather I ALWAYS QUICKLY HEAL!

EXPLETIVE DELETED – swear words and cursing send forth such an ugly, jarring energy. And this comes straight back to the originator manifesting through their life experience. Have you ever met a habitual swearer who might be described as a role model for personal happiness?

Maintaining a cool detachment is occasionally tested to the absolute limit, particularly with certain kinds of people. Walking away may seem fine in theory, yet not always the way the situation plays out for real. What to do now then? Shout and swear? Lose control and rage? Looked at from the larger point of view of quantum reality and energy balancing, that person who caused such a strong reaction from us would of course have crossed our path. How else? If we are to grow as spiritual beings to live authentically, then we are sure going to be tested until we finally get the point of the lesson.

Alternatives to expletives? OH BOTHER! OH MY! or even CRIKEY! If nothing else adopting the habit of using any of these will for sure take the sting out most situations and more than likely make both parties laugh or at the very least smile.

I DON'T WANT - followed by a statement of intent such as "...to be late" or "...to fail my interview" or "...to get greasy hair" might be anything. The point here is the sentence that starts with those three words "I don't want". If all our attention is given over to arriving late, failing the interview or indeed greasy hair, that is the energy we are sending out into universe, and confirming it perfectly with our words. Guess what is going to happen next? We will be late for that interview and fail because we had to stop on the way at the pharmacy to pick up medicated shampoo and there was a queue!

More positive statements to make here would be "I plan to leave home early then I am sure to arrive on time" or "with all my enthusiasm I stand a great chance of getting that new job" (assuming we do actually possess enthusiasm!) and "I am grateful that my hair is in great condition and I want it to stay this way".

I AM POOR - we may find ourselves temporarily low on funds from time to time, many of us have been there at some point in our lives and it rarely needs to last for long.

At one point in the mid-1990's I had all my capital invested within my new business which had yet to yield a profit. Looking in my wallet on the fourteenth of the month I saw just £10 and this was going to potentially be it until I made some more sales through the business. Thankfully I had already become used to thinking laterally so took myself off to a table-top sale in a nearby village hall and bought a box containing some oldish looking vases with that £10. I then proceeded directly to my local antiques emporium and promptly sold them on into the trade for £35, all within an hour. For nearly a year after then I became an antique trader. Buying from garage and jumble sales anything relating to pottery which seemed old and interesting, to then take them along usually the same day to my now established network of antique dealers, and happily able to usually treble or quadruple my money. As I learned more about what antique dealers look for I became more informed in my buying, reducing errors and increasing my profit. Extremely useful and welcome extra income while I waited for my main business to grow into its full potential.

Poor is a state of mind which does not serve anyone in any way. If we don't want to go through life being poor we had better quickly re-programme our mindset with more useful attitudes. There is always a way to turn-around temporary low funds through action, however leftfield that action might be. Now is the ideal time to put into practise some of the methods right here in this book to overcome any self-limiting thoughts and utilize your unique talents.

Avoid at all costs labelling yourself poor! Jettison that poor mindset forever...rather more useful is I LIVE A RICH LIFESTYLE and ensure that it is, which frequently has so truly very little to do with hard cash and is way more about attitude.

IT'S NOT MY FAULT! – making excuses for personally failing in tasks or blaming others rather than taking responsibility for our actions will inevitably bring along continually similar situations until we change that mindset to leave the negativity of passing-the-buck behind and be free. Lesson learned.

If we failed that exam we did not study hard enough. If we got overlooked for that promotion at work we did not seem like we were ready or passionate enough for it. If we did not get that hot date with the woman/man we were attracted to our approach was wrong or maybe they just do not fancy us, in which case it's time to move on. I ACCEPT RESPONSIBILITY FOR MY OWN ACTIONS.

I'M ALWAYS UNLUCKY - works as a disastrous self-fulfilling prophecy. Russell is a friend who is to all intents and purposes the luckiest man ever born. He not only won on the national lottery big time, but he also then went and did it all again within a year! Every time Russell puts a coin into a slot machine, he seems to win something. He is also able to eat like he has hollow legs and never puts on a gram in weight. He constantly tells people he is lucky with money and can eat whatever he wants, never having to worry about getting fat. A fantastic example of focus and energy in direct action. Russell is completely sincere when he makes those statements, in absolute belief he creates his own reality. Naturally, his focused energy and words give him precisely what he believes is true. Russell habitually says I AM ALWAYS LUCKY, and this mindset plays forward into his life.

I AM BORED – then quite frankly now is the time to engage with something to improve your life every single day!

Bored + lazy = disempowered living. Buy-into I LOVE IMPROVING MY LIFE.

PUTTING OTHERS DOWN - if we cannot think of a nice think to say then say nothing, as the old saying goes. Putting others down always says far more about us than the victim of our words. Would we really wish to be known as insecure and cynical? That is how those who put others down come across, every single time. And untrustworthy as well, would we impart anything of importance to someone who gossips or says negative things to us about mutual friends?

Rethinking Our Words That Are Heard

We can consistently find opportunities to refine our habitually used vocabulary. Here we are presented with such a fundamental method that anyone one of us can employ to immediately improve our quality of life in ever such a simple way. Jettisoning any words or phrases which have limited us in any sense, replacing them instead with a more positive use of language.

In addition to the few examples I have given you, I am sure when you start to focus your attention (by jotting down for a day how you express yourself) you too are going to come up with words you use which might well be limiting your potential for greatness. Those which gut instinct tells you it is time for you to lose now. Listen, pay heed, and dramatically transform the energy you surround yourself with.

Affirmations

Meditation can help here. When I first started out with affirmations a few decades ago, I did find the best time to say them was directly after a meditation. I would have a few postcards with my chosen affirmations written down on them placed by the side of me, then when I had finished my meditation, I would be in the correct mindset to contemplate saying some affirmations.

If you find, for the moment at least, you cannot get into the right mindset for affirmations (and they need to be completely relaxed and never from desperation) then best avoid using them. You really will not be doing yourself any favours and on the contrary, they can be more limiting to yourself, rather than achieving anything worthwhile.

Mindset and feeling are all that really matters to unlock the way to attract anything positive for ourselves and the words we then choose to use that reinforce that feeling. Followed by inevitably directly getting involved in the nuts and bolts of making it real when the time arrives for action.

If you are going to use affirmations you vitally need to feel the emotions first. Before a word comes of your mouth begin to build up the feelings inside of you. Build it up and build it up and build it up. This REALLY matters to me! I need this in my life, this reality in my life!!!

And only then say the affirmation...whilst still being prepared to take the necessary action that is our part of the deal!

You do not need to chant it three thousand times. Once a day is plenty with all this powerful emotion, the feeling behind those words of yours!

As I have already written more extensively about this in my book Staying Positive Regardless I am not going to suggest specific affirmations here or exact words or phrases, because I trust you will know what is relevant in your life and what will work best for you.

So far we have dealt with ways to live more on harmony with ourselves...how about experiencing amazing health as well?

Enjoying A Long And Healthy Life

Our human body is the only physical means we have at our disposal to enjoy this amazing bluey green planet of ours!

It makes perfect sense then the fewer stresses we put on our physical body and digestive system by choosing carefully what is taken into it, the easier time it is going to have.

Personally I have found during the course of the last three decades of studying how my own body reacts to what I choose to nourish it with that it functions better by giving it mostly unprocessed food. The more natural my chosen food stuff is, the smaller the list of ingredients on any kind of label gracing the packaging, the healthier and happier my body is.

Eating food free from artificial colours/sugars, flavour enhancers, e-numbers and preservatives means our delicately balanced digestive system is going to have an easier time coping with it.

So many of us tend to eat regular as clockwork and this can leave us feeling either hungry in those times when we are burning those extra calories or else overfull, because we ate when the clock told us it was time for lunch, even if we didn't actually feel like it right now.

Develop the habit of eating when hungry, rather than when the clock insists it is a mealtime. This is listening to the needs of our body and places far less stress on our digestive system.

Grazing throughout the day, eating a little often, gives our digestion an easier time by never stressing it. Further on this subject, overburdening our body and this applies even with the healthiest food or drink if we overeat, is putting unnecessary strain on our finely tuned digestive system.

Another Choice

As someone who then lived the urban life, the invitation to spend a few days staying right in the heart of the country on the poultry farm owned by extended family was an opportunity I readily jumped at.

We seldom realise beforehand those pivotal moments which happen in life, this was to be just such an experience.

Arriving late at night, the following morning I got the guided tour of the farm, consisting of shed after giant shed of caged battery-hens. Entering the first of these sheds to witness first-hand the stark reality of the confined life of these hens left me shocked and horrified. Over the next couple of days of my vacation I would occasionally venture solo to peer into the sheds, observing more closely, but only from the safety of the doorway. If you have never seen such a place, let me tell you the stench and sound is overwhelming, that combined with the sight of tens of thousands of tightly caged birds ensured I left after a few days to return to my life now resolutely vegetarian and seeking to know more.

A vegetarian diet requires about 25% of the land required to feed a meat eater annually. For a vegan it is only 20%. Of two identical areas of land, one purely for rearing cows and the other given over to vegan food, the vegan plot will feed up to five times as many people. This crop will also require a minute percentage of the water needed by the cattle, and of course, none of the methane our bovine friends produce (adding to greenhouse gasses) will be produced by that field of wheat!

Vast areas of land, including the rainforest have been or are being cleared to rear livestock to be consumed. Over half the grain produced in the world is used to feed livestock; of which but a small proportion (some estimate as low as just 10%) could instead be used to feed all of us across the world.

Having become established as a vegetarian, I later graduated to vegan and am presently macrobiotic vegan, through listening to my own intuition during a recent journey to self-healing.

I attribute much of my ongoing wellbeing to also becoming entirely free of sugar or artificial sugars in my diet, more of which shortly.

I drink plenty of water (but not too much) and get plenty of exercise. If I cannot get out and take a walk (my favourite form of exercise) I do at least ensure to make the effort to have a 15-20-minute aerobic work-out with weights at home every day. A few years ago, I decided it would be a good idea to take myself off to my chosen healthcare provider and get a full physical. As a validation to myself I am doing things right. Imagine my delight when she told me I have the physiology and level of fitness of a healthy twenty-five-year-old (I am not twenty-five, by the way).

Brown Rice

This does have a bit of an image problem here in the West, I get that. Brown rice has become a little synonymous with VW campervans, the tie-dyed hippie movement and free love. I love hippies by the way, I have been called The Hippie Holistic Coach by the press on more than one occasion due to my uncompromisingly holistic approach to life and more than likely my bohemian appearance. The simple truth is that pure brown rice can genuinely benefit one and all. In the Far East brown rice is an essential part of the diet.

This ancient grain is one of the purest foods we can eat. Naturally high in fibre, brown rice still contains all those essential vitamins and minerals which get removed when it is processed to make white rice.

I recommend this staple of a macrobiotic diet, regardless of your own dietary lifestyle. Brown rice added into weekly meal plans ensures you are taking into your body one of the most natural foodstuffs on the planet.

Eating not only brown rice, but other natural grains such as whole-wheat, rye and barley and avoiding refined white flour or synthetically processed foodstuff, ensures we are taking the purest food into our bodies. Combine these with fresh vegetables, beans and pulses, we then eat as holistically as possible.

Vitamins

We all have easy access to just about every and any type of possible vitamin, mineral or supplement conceived of or imagined. All we need to do is hit the high street or click a mouse. Yet how many of these vits do we genuinely need to be taking and how many are simply passing through our bodies serving little useful purpose or even physically harming us?

During the last thirty years or so I confess, as a health aware vegan, I must have sampled at one time or another pretty much every one of the myriads of different vitamin and mineral concoctions available; the promised goal being to replace the essential elements vegans apparently miss out on through avoiding meat, dairy and fish.

The message here is vits are easily obtainable and we can all self-diagnose. If you do genuinely feel you could use some extra vitamins over and above your usual diet, take the time to go and get checked out by your chosen healthcare provider. That way you are sure to only be supplementing with vits or minerals you genuinely need short term. Then take the care to look at what could be added into your diet for the long-term fix.

If you are veggie or vegan, it is almost mandatory to have your B vits checked periodically as a matter of course and for peace of mind. A nicely balanced diet might well render further supplementation obsolete.

The other point we need to bear in mind is our needs are more than likely going to be entirely different during the summer months as opposed to winter; again, if your instinct is suggesting you would benefit from supplementation, a visit to your choice of healthcare provider allows you to know for sure. Facts when it comes to our wellbeing are always preferable to guesswork!

Sugars

So finally we arrive at the subject of sugar, the avoidance of which in any form has become one of my own personal passions.

I need to qualify before we start this section I am not a nutritionist, and whilst we all need to develop the habit of listening to the needs of our own bodies, nevertheless before contemplating any extreme dietary changes it is wise to firstly consult your chosen healthcare provider.

And now back to sugar...

Too many refined, artificial or even natural sugars, which are added into thousands of the things we eat, is asking a lot from our bodies to be able to absorb these alien substances which have only really become such a high percentage content of our diets in the last fifty or sixty years.

There's an excellently researched book called Sugar Blues by William Dufty, although written in the 1970's, its continued relevance today cannot be understated. If serious about wellbeing I do recommend you read this or a similar book.

Sugar causes highs and lows in our moods. And so many of us are quite unaware of just how many refined sugars we are taking into our bodies every single day. Sugar is added to practically every single processed food. Even if you think you might well be enjoying a low-sugar diet, check out all those ingredients and you will find virtually everything does indeed contain sugar or artificial sugar concealed under one name or another.

A FEW COMMONLY USED NAMES FOR SUGARS AND SUGAR ALTERNATIVES – Aspartame, Syrup, Fructose, Saccharin, Sucralose, Sorbitol, Glycerol, Dextrose, Concentrated Fruit Juice, Galactose, Corn Syrup, Ethyl Maltol, Glucose Syrup, Maltodextrin and Barley Malt; there are literally hundreds of other chemical and e-numbers manufacturers of foodstuff and cosmetics use in place of simply stating sugar on their list of ingredients.

Sugar gives us that familiar high. It contains no nutritional value whatsoever, but it certainly does give us a high. That energy rush, unfortunately shortly afterwards comes the crash. Then we feel lacking in energy. Yet not only does sugar affect us physically, it also directly influences our moods.

Wendy felt incredibly down and lacking in motivation a lot of the time. Digging down together into her life revealed nothing of any real consequence which might be causing her to feel this way. She had no health issues or stresses beyond what most of us experience. I followed my intuition to suggest to Wendy she might like to adjust her diet for a minimum of two weeks by cutting out as much sugar and artificial sugar as she felt comfortably able to. She duly reported back after this fortnight that she felt like her life had been transformed, experiencing a sense of being so much more in control of her emotional wellbeing and balanced within her moods.

Really ponder sugar, research it online - but first a word of caution. Be sure to read from reputable sources, a fair percentage of the online 'research' relating to sugar has been rather sneakily funded by a certain globally high-profile soft drink manufacturer. Not exactly unbiased advice!

Then if you agree with me, that sugar is not something which ought to be part of your diet – start to gradually reduce your sugar level. Don't go cold-turkey and cut it completely out of your diet, gently easing away from sugar will put far less stress on your body.

As part of my own healing journey a little while ago I decided overnight to abruptly adopt a no sugar and free-from artificial sugar lifestyle. Convinced as I personally was, through paying attention to clues from my body, that sugar had contributed greatly to the health issues I found myself dealing with. This left me with little choice, I had to go cold-turkey. Having experienced that particular rollercoaster I can tell you that gradually reducing our sugar intake is for sure the gentler way of doing things!

If you too go sugar free you are going to soon feel the difference in your life. There will be a period of withdrawal, stay with it anyway and persist until your body is cleared of all those processed sugars.

I wake in the morning energized and have the most amazingly balanced moods/emotions I have experienced at any time in my life.

Organic

There is organic produced food and then there is ethically produced organic food.

Some of the animal waste based organic fertilizers, such as chicken pellet manure commercially used by growers and directly available to us via garden stores, has been produced as a by-product of factory farming in one form or another. This might be okay for many people, however, with the broader picture of ethics taken into consideration feeding our plants with the by-product of a brutally efficient system of farming can hardly help us to grow happy botanical specimens.

The same applies with pesticides. Rather than drenching our food in chemicals like most commercial growers do, there are more natural ways of doing things. Permaculture is one example, the planting of sympathetic plants to protect one another from likely pests. Using essential oils such as citronella as a repellent to avoid crops being eaten by insects or lavender to discourage weeds are becoming more widespread. There is a wealth of reliable information on the internet from organizations such as The Soil Association and some version of the Organic Consumers Network exists in one form or another in most countries.

If you are buying most of your foodstuffs in from grocery stores a little personal investigation into where their products come from and how they are grown can pay dividends. Alternatively, growing your own fruit and vegetables puts you in control of what products go onto them and happily there are a wealth of ethical organic options out there, either for fertilizing or pest control.

We are products of our daily habits...

Finding Good Enough Reasons To Avoid Self-Inflicted Poisons

As we have already established, us humans are creatures of habit. And unless we get some kind of clarion wake up call, the chances are whatever neural pathways we have taken years to establish will continue to run the same programmes and patterns throughout our lives.

Many people do indeed spend small fortunes to self-inflict pollution upon their bodies in full knowledge of the potential negative side effects of their choice.

The only reason why any of us continue with an action which is clearly against our own self-interest is because we have not yet given ourselves a sufficiently good enough reason to not do!

Please understand that I am not judging anyone's actions here. I am a passionate advocate of our right to complete freedom of choice, obviously as long our actions harm no others. And yet paradoxically some of the lifestyle choices we make for ourselves do indeed unintentionally have an all too real and sometimes devastating effect on those who love and care about us.

I feel particularly motivated to encourage any of you who do buy-into one or more of the following health-defeating lifestyle choices to look within yourself for your personal **Good Enough Reason** to change. Get your inner health mojo working in your behalf in your own life.

Every one of us already knows about all the self-inflicted poisons we are talking about here. My wish is that we all now collectively achieve a different level of personal understanding through talking candidly about them.

I need to add if you are addicted to any of these self-inflicted poisons be sure to take the advice of your chosen healthcare provider before making any changes; there is so much support and help available, take it all if you feel that you need it!

During each section I will detail one or two of my own personal **Good Enough Reasons** and suggest some emotional levers you can also use to bring a new paradigm to transform an old habit.

Smoking

I am a bit of a non-smoker; well okay I have never felt inclined to ever try it. As I mentioned, I am passionate about the freedom to make our own decisions, mine has been to avoid tobacco. I have personally always disliked the aroma of smoking, which was been enough to put me off ever wanting to become a smoker. Throughout childhood I would not eat if someone nearby smoked, and to be honest I still feel the same way today.

It has been known for certainly all my lifetime that smoking is hardly beneficial to health in any way. On the contrary it can create as a by-product its own range of serious problems and issues with the ingested carcinogens. I believe we are all responsible for our own actions and in these times in which we live everyone is fully aware of the health risks involved in choosing to smoke. The packaging on tobacco carries brutally graphic illustrations of the damage we inflict upon our bodies when smoking, but this alone is not enough to persuade the passionate smoker to quit.

We all need Good Enough Reasons to change a habitual behaviour. If you are doing everything else right and still smoking you already know you are making your body work so much harder to clear the associated toxins.

Cigarettes do also contain sugar, this surprises many people, they can indeed have a remarkably high sugar content, up to 20% in fact. Clearly the health hazards needing to be considered relating to a high sugar intake as well!

My own mother had not smoked for well over two decades, but unfortunately as a previously heavy smoker the damage was already done. She died last year due to (amongst a few other secondary issues) complications from years of smoking; even though she had not touched a cigarette for so long. I can confirm having been alongside her all the way during this journey that death due to smoking will be agonisingly slow and excruciatingly painful.

At an event I met a woman in her early twenties who during her lifetime had witnessed her great grandmother, great grandfather, grandmother, and tragically both of her parents all die due to smoking related cancers and bizarrely she also smoked! Clearly, she had yet to encounter her own personal Good Enough Reason to make a new choice. No matter how much logic and common sense says otherwise or the emotional pain we experience, we are more than able to turn a blind eye to changing habitual behaviours so deeply embedded within our neural pathways.

The most effective way to transform any poor habit is to link pain or self-ridicule to it.

Take some photos of yourself smoking, really study these photos to see how incongruous with living a long and healthy life this action is.

In most first world countries being a smoker in winter means standing outside in all weathers every time you feel the need to indulge. Take photos of this as well! Standing outside there shivering in minus temperatures or trying to shelter from gale force winds and icy rain as you are enjoying a smoke. Then see for yourself how switched on and intelligent you look...

Volunteer at your local hospice, freely giving of your time to help others, whilst also witnessing first-hand the far from beautiful final period of life endured by those with cancer caused by smoking.

We will go more into how crucial it is to replace any poor life-choices with something more pleasurable at the end of the chapter...in the meantime, let's talk...

Alcohol

Often considered fine in moderation, some health experts even going so far as to suggest that a glass of excellent quality organic red wine or beer is health beneficial. A good rule of thumb here is if we avoid overburdening our body with anything that requires a recovery time from eating or drinking we are on the right track.

During my brief encounter with the biggest publishing company in town during my first job, I met two engagingly witty salesmen, Tim and Larry. They were both kind to my sixteen-year-old self and spending some time laughing with them certainly brightened the few dull weeks I spent at that company. After I left we still crossed paths occasionally, but sadly not for too long. Tim and Larry were both functioning alcoholics; they had seemed old to me when I was sixteen, but in reality were only in their mid-forties when liver disease claimed both of them within a few months of one another. Consequently, since then, my personal association with alcohol etched into my belief system is the premature ending of life. My **Good Enough Reason** is an over-riding emotion relating to alcohol that it robs us of authentically living life to the full, as epitomized in the case of my two late friends whose intellect had burned so brightly.

The guy finally gets that long sought-after promotion at work. Or perhaps he is about to get married the next day. Cue taking on-board industrial quantities of alcohol to celebrate the occasion. This one has mystified me for years, surely some awesome news worth celebrating is a time to savour. Rather than making it an occasion we will more than likely not actually remember or perhaps would even prefer to forget...

To change any habit we need to transform the emotional way we view it, how it makes us feel. Having photos of ourselves to reflect upon are wonderfully eye-opening!

As I suggested with smoking, if you habitually over-indulge in alcohol be sure to take plenty of selfie photos during the process of becoming inebriated. The following day take a good long look to study just how you looked and behaved during the previous evening.

Better still take some photos of how awesome you look waking first thing in the morning after that heavy night before! When you are on your way for another night-out keep one particularly stinking photo of what alcohol does to you as the home-screen on your phone as a poignant reminder to yourself.

We only need to check-out any news blog or newspaper to read of the latest family to have been devastated by alcohol, maybe through a drunk-driver or someone passing away far before their time (as with my two friends) due to liver damage.

If you drink every day it is worth considering that you could well have an issue with alcohol. To confirm this go for three days without touching an alcoholic drink. If this is a struggle or turns out to be impossible, seek out what support or help is available locally.

Junk Food

This is not called junk for nothing! An occasional junky indulgence our bodies can just about cope with. Living off the stuff constantly is inevitably self-damaging. Deep fried food is universally recognised by nutritional experts as increasing the likelihood of heart disease, high cholesterol and diabetes. Moderation or avoidance all together must be the sensible option for any of us interested in a long and healthy life.

Food products are generally advertised in terms of the lifestyle that eating them will offer. Not too much attention on the product, it is far more about the cool happy people in the adverts who are having a wonderful life, and all because they eat the advertised food or soft drink.

I met Shane after he had already suffered a serious heart attack, he was now burdened with diabetes and grossly overweight. His career as a commercial pilot far behind him through his physical health issues, nevertheless Shane still found it challenging to eat healthily, claiming junky food gave him pleasure. Frankly seeing where his eating habits had taken him it was more challenging for his family and friends to understand exactly what pleasure he derived...we all have a choice.

Junk food is packed full of flavour enhancers such as MSG, e-numbers, sugar in its myriad of forms, and artificial colours to make it look more attractive. Is it any wonder wholefoods and the more natural dietary options can seem a little bland comparatively? We need to reset our tastebuds. If we do this then after a short while purer eating will begin to taste delicious.

As a teenager I too indulged in junky delights,. I can confirm that gradually transforming the way we eat does indeed also change the way we taste food in a positive sense. I guess you will have to give this one a go to experience it!

My **Good Enough Reason** came through the irrefutable visual evidence of how my energy levels increased, and the way my skin and hair looked after cutting out poor quality foodstuffs by switching over to a more natural way of eating.

In youth our bodies recover from over-indulgence in poor foodstuffs quickly, although the results are generally still there in dermatological evidence or cholesterol levels. It bears remembering that according to Zen every front will have a back, therefore if we spend our youth eating and drinking junk, somewhere further down our timeline payback day will arrive. This could manifest as later in life being faced with serious health issues that we now need to deal with, those which might well have been easily avoided with different lifestyle choices earlier.

If you know your diet consists of a greater proportion of highly processed or junk food why not take yourself off to your chosen healthcare provider for a full physical examination? Ask them to not only test for the usual stuff such as cholesterol, body mass index and vit levels; also find out the condition and real-time age of your skin through dermatological profiling and your level of physical fitness.

Recreational Drugs

Offering an artificial form of escapism. Regular users of recreational drugs will claim their habit does them no harm. Medical statistics would say otherwise. Long-term use of recreational drugs can affect us through psychological issues such as creating paranoia, difficulty in concentrating and if over-used even death!

There is a tradition within artistic and creative endeavours for some people to use so called soft drugs as a means to access alternative ways of expanding their consciousness (as shamans traditionally also do to enter other realms). Yet how real are the results of all this artificially induced music or art? The guy who cannot get artistically inspired without taking drugs must not be naturally a creative type of person...meditation equally also allows us to expand our conscious awareness...

Far too many amazing singers and actors have been lost to drugs. All the commercial success they attained and adulation of the public failed to fulfil their emotional needs and they chose to ease their pain through drugs.

If you have children and want to raise awareness in them about the reality of drugs get them involved in donating food or clothing to a drug rehab centre. Make it your family centred project, then all of you visit the centre to personally give them your donation, allow your children to see first-hand the stark reality of drug use.

If you are a creative person who extensively uses drugs as part of your artistic process I am going to get a bit in your face to call you out and challenge you right now to see what you can produce without any artificial high. You might well surprise yourself...

Caffeine

Gives us an energy rush, increases heartbeat and too much caffeine causes stomach upsets. In my corporate days I would regularly drink over twenty cups of coffee a day! Not surprisingly I suffered from insomnia and irritability daily. A routine blood-test showed up practically caffeine running through my veins, definitely my overdue wake-up call and **Good Enough Reason** to adopt an instant new paradigm!

Too much caffeine risks many more possible side-effects than we can cover here, you will all know the ones we are talking about – those including kidney issues, high blood pressure; and painful withdrawal symptoms such as cluster headaches.

I recently enjoyed a detailed conversation with a brain surgeon who stated that neither he or any of his colleagues choose to drink coffee or caffeine rich drinks. Enough validation for any of us against using caffeine I would say...

You Deserve To Feel Awesome!

Feeling personally motivated is essential to make any kind of change in our lives. We need to link pain or better still self-ridicule related to continuing with our existing paradigm. I cannot tell you exactly what's going to push your own buttons, you are going to have to work that one out for yourself...

What we can all do though when deeply desiring to transform away from indulging in any type of action we unconditionally know makes no sense at all (such as intentionally self-poisoning) is to firstly get our inner health mojo working for us.

And secondly replace the negative action with something awesome we would love to do instead.

This feel-good action can be anything that feels amazing to you; walking in nature, making love, getting a pet, spending quality time with family, studying something new, taking up woodwork, origami, writing poetry, volunteering of our time, going to the gym, swimming, travel, cooking deliciously healthy meals, running or meditating.

When we actually improve our quality of life by taking on something new we love to do as part of the process of discarding an old paradigm we gift ourselves the best possible opportunity for our desired changes to stick.

Exercising Our Right To Exercise

If you follow the steps in this book comfort zones are going to be left behind and for sure there will be days when stress makes itself known. The fitter you are, the easier you will find yourself able to cope and enjoy the ride.

Practically all my fellow coaches take regular exercise, they are convinced this a major contributor to their effectiveness and the longevity of some of their careers. There are indeed several high-profile lifestyle coaches, who although well into their seventies and some even their eighties, still regularly conduct seminars and write relevant new books.

Body Breakdown Reversal

As our body matures it is usual for it to start losing muscle mass, to be replaced with fat or muscle wastage, resulting in less physical strength and suppleness.

It does not have to be this way, not at all.

The only reason for this loss of muscle mass is due to a lack of aerobic and anaerobic exercise - our brain then receives the message that we are not using our muscles in the way we once did and concludes we must no longer require them. Kick-starting the beginning of the transformational changes in our bodies commonly recognised to be signs of old age.

Yet paradoxically there are many examples of lean and mean octogenarians who are still superbly fit and leading the kind of active lives that would put many of their grandchildren to shame.

What is the difference here, what can possibly be their miraculous secret?

In virtually all these cases those individuals have always led active lives and saw no reason to slow down or stop doing what they have always done simply because another birthday passed on by. As a result of this they have kept a good high percentage of their muscle mass throughout their life.

Getting Out What We Put In

Exercise is crucially important for maintaining a healthy body and strengthening our immune system's ability to fend off disease and decay. Investing in ourselves in terms of eating healthily and partaking of regular exercise is going to be more than worth the effort later down our timeline when we can still run up the stairs and experience life to the full.

I spent my time in gyms back in the day and for sure they can be an excellent starting place when venturing into getting fit for perhaps the first time in years. Any good gym will have qualified instructors to advise you on taking those first steps. It is vital to start gently at first. If you realistically know you are extremely unfit it is certainly prudent to consult a health professional before beginning to make any changes.

Regular gentle exercise is always preferable to doing nothing at all, and you can always increase the length and intensity of your work out once you start to gain enough fitness to safely feel more able.

Small steps towards our goals are preferable to none every single time!

Never Need To Diet

It seems every week a new miracle diet hits the headlines, with the usual promise of quick weight-loss by buying-into their selected new eating regime.

Give or take a kilo, I have weighed the same for the past three decades. This is not because I might not be inclined to put weight on, it is all down to firstly eating holistically with an eye to my long-term wellbeing. And secondly, also making sure my lifestyle includes plenty of aerobic exercise for fitness and some anaerobic exercise for muscle mass.

Rather than buying into yo-yo dieting, complete tailored lifestyles for holistic wellbeing gives you or I the best chance possible of maintaining our perfect weight long-term.

We are what we focus attention upon, what we think about and say makes our reality. If we are there spending every day desperately obsessing on the need to lose weight and frequently glancing in the mirror underlines this, for sure we need to adjust our mindset to then experience the difference this makes. If all we constantly think about is losing weight, we will constantly have weight to lose – adopting a new mindset will prove significantly more effective and work more permanently than any diet. We need to re-apply our attention on building our **lifestyle** around actively becoming our vision of how we see our ideal physical self.

We empower ourselves by opting to turbo-charge our weight loss goals with the right mindset; and consequently designing a tailored lifestyle to bring ourselves to where we desire to be physically, this is the only skill-set needed to achieve genuine permanent weight loss.

This is so easy as well!

Quite simply cut out of your new lifestyle anything at all which is incongruous with how your vision of the way your ideal self looks. Instead choosing to focus all your attention on only things such as tastily fantastically healthy food/drink and regular exercise. Find an exercise you can buy-into to really enjoy, this can be anything from dancing, yoga, swimming, martial arts, running, Zumba, hill trekking or taking part in a sport, something you can look forward to doing, and can so easily be integrated into your weekly routine.

Make this choice right now and you bring this vision of your ideal physical self so much closer into genuinely being your long-term reality. Quite rapidly you will see the results manifesting for you, ensuring your lasting motivation to carry right on all the way through to finally living the life you deserve and feeling good about your mirror image...

Our Nature To Be Found In Nature

Nature is good for the soul. Our ancestors lived a life much closer to nature. They were aware of the passing seasons and how to read coming weather changes.

Is it any wonder given our usual fast-forward lifestyle that so many people in the 21st century have lost an inherent spirituality? I am not necessarily talking about organised religion here. I mean more looking within ourselves and thinking about who we fundamentally are. Our connection to the infinite. Why we here on this planet at this moment...

We deserve to engage with life to the full and enjoy every single day, whatever twists and turns it might take, remaining true to our own ethics and moral code.

Enjoying some fun, which might well cost absolutely nothing in hard cash, but is nevertheless priceless. Now that is really living!

- Think of walking in a forest after a fresh shower of rain, those heady scents combined with the sound of birdsong high above in the trees.
- Sitting by a seashore as roaring waves crash in on the beach or perhaps soothingly lap gently onto the shoreline.
- The beauty of taking in the awe-inspiring wonder of a meadow resplendent with a kaleidoscope of wildflowers.
- The drama of a wild thunderstorm.
- Looking up as an eagle majestically soars against a stunning sunset.
- To be out on a crisp winters evening, the sky purest black and a million stars twinkling like diamonds.

- Or a scorching hot summer's day, feeling the sun warming upon our backs and experiencing true contentment.

This is real life.

This is directly appreciating freely given beauty, the beauty of nature, of our own natures; and it is all waiting right there as it has always been. Waiting for you and me to feel it through all our senses, with every breath down through every atom of our very being!

So, what would you rather enjoy?

Any one of these amazing natural experiences or spending time on your smartphone?

Why not go and take a walk instead?

Living 24/7 in completely artificial environments stifles creativity and deadens our intuition. Creating an uninspired zombie-like worker drone level of existence.

If you are one of those people who doesn't usually have the time for nature or perhaps even finds the prospect of exploring wilderness areas scary, how about you take only half an hour a couple of times a week to visit your local public park?

Simply sit and observe. Leave aside the headphones and no cheating yourself out of the experience by talking or texting on your phone!

Look at the trees, the grass and then listen. Hear birdsong? Do the trees make a noise? Rustling poplars or creaking old oaks. Breathe in the scents. Soak up the sights, sounds and smells, feel on every level what it is like to be there.

Like we cannot step into the same water of a river twice, every time we visit nature it will be different.

Slowly, but surely, your awareness of nature will grow more acute through these visits to the park. At some point maybe even venturing a little further outside your town or city to explore some more untamed nature. Then again, perhaps you are already very connected to nature and cannot relate in any way to this section so far, living as you do in the country or on the edge of an area of wilderness.

Oh, you can help so many people!

Invite your town or city family and friends to come over to stay with you as often as possible. Show them your reality. Take them outside and allow them to learn to appreciate the joy of nature through your eyes. Be their guide and show them how beautiful nature is in all her manifestations.

Exercise in nature is my first choice every time. Walking, running or tai chi within a natural setting is far from simply only taking exercise – it is wonderfully inspirational. Most of my game-changing ideas have popped into my head way out in the wilderness or in the middle of a deserted ancient Neolithic site. Rarely do I feel connected to nature enough to feel inspired in the middle of a busy city...

As I lead a fairly public life, my way of finding some battery re-charging time is taking myself off for an all-day solo coastal walk or deep down into the forest. This is especially effective in the heart of winter when the harsh weather discourages many others from venturing outside. It is for sure a challenge in this era in which we live to find ourselves some true seclusion. I have to say though, a gale force wind and driving rain usually means I am going to enjoy having the beach pretty much to myself and with the magical bonus of making me feel wonderfully alive, leaving me with a heart full of gratitude for nature in all her extremes.

Take the time to take some time out for you – there is always a way.

A Mindful Approach To Health

There is an old saying - image, ordain and manifest.

In other words, think about something deeply, keeping that image strongly focused there in your mind. Then say it out loud and the energy wave transmitted makes it happen for you. And it still holds 100% true.

Phil's greatest fear was losing his mind. Having witnessed his much older brother succumb to dementia, Phil dreaded the horror of his own life following the same path. Although he was perfectly fit, ate for optimum health and led an extremely active lifestyle, he nevertheless fixated upon the unlikely chance of developing a similar illness. For sure his brother had died through this illness but this hardly compelled Phil to also go ahead and experience the same fate. By fixate I mean he read everything there is to know about the subject, often verbally expressing just how much he did not want to get the illness or lose his mental faculties.

Sure enough he did eventually find his life turned upside down. Phil did not get dementia, sadly though he did develop a benign but inoperable brain tumour. With only a few short months of life ahead of him, Phil did finally have the opportunity to make the connection between the thoughts of fear he had vocalised for years and where he now found himself. Did Phil's thoughts attract his illness? He told me he was certainly convinced they had...

At the other end of the scale, the energy from our own thoughts can bring about little miracles.

Another guy I know also found himself diagnosed with a growth in his brain. He first noticed it due to persistent headaches and cognitive challenges manifesting as quite noticeable short-term memory issues. Eventually taking himself off to get checked by his chosen healthcare provider revealed a colloid cyst lodged in the centre of his brain. Three separate specialists in turn had 'the conversation' with him, explaining the position of the cyst meant it would be inoperable, inevitably it would grow and eventually lead to sudden death with no warning.

Our guy quit work for a while, not to wait for his imminent demise, but rather to work on himself every single day through meditation, refining his dietary input and visioning living a future of his own choice, free from pain or limitation. It took three years of continuously empowering mindsets as he gradually re-gained all his cognitive faculties, his once poor short-term memory now fully functioning again, the debilitating cluster headaches passed to never return. He leads a significantly fuller and richer life than ever before his diagnosis; and with a renewed passion for experiencing new things wherever and whenever possible.

All Healing Is Essentially Self-Healing

If we go along the conventional route to health, taking ourselves off to a GP and embracing orthodox medicine, it is still essentially our own body which is healing for itself. Prescribed drugs or medication simply will not work if we believe they are not going to be effective. Conversely there have been well documented cases of individuals making full recoveries from illnesses or injury, while having been taking nothing more than a placebo pill, their trust in its effectiveness being strong enough to bring about healing.

Our mind is immensely powerful and possesses infinite capabilities to heal our bodies...we simply need reminding how and then we can grow into our full potential. In the rest of this chapter I will show you some naturally holistic techniques to deal with a few of life's little health challenges.

I do need to add a word of sensible caution before we carry on, obviously these techniques are never intended to act as a substitute for the attention of your chosen healthcare provider. If you are feeling persistently unwell do seek professional help.

The 30 Second De-Stress

I want to give you something which, although never intended as a long-term cure, represents a more instant way of just taking ourselves away from a stressful situation, calming things down to re-centre and look at whatever we need to deal with more within context.

Perhaps it is just one of those days, one challenge after another has presented itself and we feel like we are about to go pop!

The 30 Second De-Stress

- Sit still and close your eyes.
- Concentrate on the colours you can see behind your eyelids, even if this is only black, no rules here. Whatever colours you see is fine.

- In your mind start to count slowly back from 30 to 0.
- 30 (pause and breathe) 29 (pause and breathe) 28 (pause and breathe) 27 and so on, until you eventually reach 0.
- When you have arrived down at 0, you can open your eyes.

Many people, from all walks of life, have found this simple little exercise incredibly useful. It is something I have been teaching for well over twenty years and everybody who has adopted it into their lifestyle has found some degree of benefit from it.

The beauty is the 30 Second Destress can be practiced almost anywhere at any time. I mean clearly when it is safe to do so – if you are driving please find somewhere safe to park-up first or if operating heavy machinery do move away before using this exercise!

On a more serious note though, feel free to share this once you have proved to yourself that it works. The more people who know about the 30 Second De-Stress the sooner we can collectively bring a little more peace into this World…

By taking this opportunity to go within ourselves for a few moments we psychologically disconnected from the immediate cause of the stress there before us. Like I suggested this is never intended to be a long-term cure, what it does though is place our personal power back into our own hands, rather than feeling events are running out of control. When feeling more centred we are for sure able to deal with any possible challenges we find ourselves presented with in a level-headed way.

When teaching others my primary aim is for my audiences or clients to be able to quickly take complete control of their own lives and destiny. What would be the point in anyone relying on someone else to solve all their issues for them whenever a challenge in life happens along? Far better we all develop the inner strength and confidence in our own ability to deal with whatever crosses our path.

Insomnia

Sleep is essential if we are to function to the best of our ability. Sleeping when we feel tired if possible. Sleep is regenerating.

When suffering from insomnia, and we have probably all been there at some point, for sure I have...it can seem unending! There are some methods we can use which will help us have a good night's sleep.

- A crucial step is to avoid coffee or any caffeine rich drinks for at least four hours before retiring for bed. Drink something else instead, chamomile tea is excellent, very relaxing. Have a chamomile tea an hour or so before you are contemplating retiring for the night.

- Take a warm shower. Leave aside any invigorating shower gels, instead something more relaxing to put you in a chilled mood. A nice warm shower, with calming shower gel will place you more in the mindset for sleep.

- Essential oils can help as well. Never put them directly on your skin. Place a few drops of lavender essential oil (if you like the aroma) on a handkerchief or tissue, put this under your pillow where you are still able to smell it, but it is not overpowering, helps the mind get into a more relaxed ready-for-sleep state.

- I have found one of the methods which works well for me is to hypnotise myself to sleep. Which in my case is to start at one thousand and gradually slowly count backwards to zero in my head. I do generally find long before I have even reached back to nine hundred, I am fast asleep!

Relationships

If our relationship is the cause of stress, honesty with how we are feeling and frankly communicating this is so freeing. Especially if this can be talked about without resentment or hostility.

Firstly, we need to be honest with ourselves about what we truly feel. And once we have gone through the process of searching within, we can begin to share this. Let's face it if our relationship is the cause of feeling stressed, then in all likelihood our partner is going through a similar reality and will welcome the opportunity for dialogue.

Sitting down and talking with one another is the beginning to resolution. Resentment can build up through a lack of communication and if everyone knows exactly where they are then at last some kind resolution can happen. You can both transparently see where the relationship is going to go and how to move forward.

Keep talking to one another, even if these discussions happen over the course of several days or even weeks; seek counselling if you mutually believe it will help. Talking can potentially bring you closer, as you understand one another's needs a little better now. Then again, if you collectively reach the conclusion that the relationship is genuinely not fixable then you can both amicably let it go, allowing each other to be happy elsewhere.

Headaches

Wouldn't it be rather wonderful if there were a truly holistic way to self-heal headaches? Often related to stress, but certainly not always, headaches can be one of the trickiest maladies to self-heal. After all we need to be able to focus our attention to help ourselves and a challenging pain in our own head is clearly going to make this a particular challenge to overcome.

As one who used to find myself subject to headaches regularly and unwilling to simply pop a pill to ease the discomfort, I sought out a method to help myself whenever the need presented itself. And one which by obvious necessity did not require many hours of focussed concentration or meditation on my own part.

Find somewhere quiet to sit, with no bright lights to distract you or electronic gadgetry in your proximity.

- Close your eyes and intensely focus your attention directly on the area of pain (don't worry, this won't be for long!).
- Strongly imagine the pain of your headache as a grey cloud floating outward from your forehead, to hover in the air a metre in front of you.
- Your headache pain, now floating in the air right there on level with your head a metre away.
- Then watch as it slowly commences moving away from you, drifting away into the distance until you can no longer see it.
- Open your eyes, if you have done this right, you will be feeling considerably more at ease now.

I need to add that this method is obviously not infallible and if you are experiencing persistent headaches please do take yourself off to your chosen healthcare provider to get assessed.

I have to say this is another one of the most popular self-healing techniques I teach, giving people their own ability to treat their headaches has proved invaluable to them.

Pain

Dealing with pain from a physical injury or specific pain in an isolated area of our own body works by precisely the same methodology as the previous section on headaches.

- In the same way as with our headache, strongly tune-into the epicentre of the pain to FEEL the discomfort.
- Then image it as a grey cloud lifting away from the area of your body which the epicentre of the pain is centred, to float a metre or so in front of you...
- And as before, the grey cloud then drifts away to eventually disappear.

If you have a persistent injury it may well be useful to practise a healing session per day for as long as it takes to dissipate entirely.

Like with the headache healing, here we helped ourselves by taking the element of a localized pain; and symbolizing it as a grey cloud moved it outside of our body.

Holistic Therapies

There are a whole range of therapies which can help us relax more to deal with stress and emotional blockages.

An aromatherapy massage is wonderfully soothing. Most towns have an aromatherapy clinic, find one with all the official certifications and insurance hanging on the wall and book a session. You will surely feel better for the experience, and it costs extraordinarily little proportional to the relaxation achieved.

Acupuncture and acupressure work on the meridians of the body, releasing any emotional energy blockages which could be causing our physical symptoms. Deep tissue massage and reflexology are infinitely calming.

It is worth the effort for seeking out an alternative therapy which speaks to you, if sensing you could benefit from a little outside help. Recommendation are always the preferred way to choose a therapist or counsellor, ask friends or look online to know more about a particular therapy or practitioner.

Part Two

Your Labour Of Love

Sometimes life gives us a big flashing neon sign.
"Step this way please, now is the time!"
Needing to be ready to act, seems illogical, feeling wary.
Take that action, embracing change, no matter how scary.
Finally on the way to living our life how it should be.
When opportunities come along, embracing our destiny.

Introduction

We have all experienced those moments, especially in childhood playing and also often in adult daydreaming, where we can clearly visualize ourselves doing a certain job and living a certain kind of life. Yet how many of us choose to follow what destiny was calling us towards?

I saw myself as a writer or perhaps an educator of some kind. After a lengthily steep learning curve my personal choices eventually enabled me to work within both of my dreams, by firstly making them achievable **goals**. I contribute to over thirty magazines worldwide each year, as I travel to give radio and television interviews or live talks in my seminars I am teaching as much as I could have ever wished.

If a dream is in any way possible to feasibly happen for you…however remote or abstract it may be…then you can empower yourself to achieve that dream…by making it a goal!

We may personally love the idea of saving lives, which is of course entirely possible within an incredible variety of different career options; whilst our friend might have alternatively only ever have wished to pilot the first intergalactic space shuttle, which on the face of it appears to be realistically impossible - unless they make it their reality by becoming an actor...there is always a way!

Now Is The Time!

What time is it? By the time you looked at your watch or phone it was already too late...

In the moment I asked you what time it was that very second had already gone, therefore whatever answer you gave me had to be wrong.

The same question asked with knowledge of quantum reality can only have one answer. Now!

Now is the only possible moment.

When you started to read the line above the end of it was in your future. When you finished the line, the beginning was then in your past. You though existed in both of those moments and hopefully still do! While you were in the process of reading it, you existed only in the now. Every moment is in fact...Now.

It is the same with our bodies and the essence of us some call spirit, soul or higher self. The cells of our bodies contain a memory of everything that has happened to us and indeed an imprint for probable future events. And yet, as humans, the only possible time zone we exist in is now.

What if it were possible for us to change the way we feel about ourselves? Could we then go on to create a completely different future?

Yes! It is possible to shape our own destiny and then our life can take an entirely different direction.

Through changing our mindset of what is possible from our lives, our future can then be entirely in our own hands to create whatever reality we desire.

Be A Helicopter Pilot!

An airplane needs a lengthy runway to take off. Our helicopter can take off vertically, just as we can when we say YES to those frequently unexpected opportunities which come along taking us straight up to a completely new level of success.

The airplane needs half the sky to change direction. Our helicopter can change direction instantly, just as we can continually adapt to whichever direction our intuition is telling us we need to go next.

This same airplane requires a long runway to land. Our helicopter can hover and land anywhere which seems interesting, just as it is valuable for us to stop occasionally to see the bigger picture, which might lead to us choosing to touch base with awesome new experiences.

Let us all be helicopter pilots in life!

You Only Need To See The Next Step

Attempting to meticulously work out how to practically take every single action beforehand to get from the point you are now all the way through to where you desire to eventually be is virtually impossible, and anyway you would miss out on all the fun!

As repetition gives the best chance for any changes in mindset to stick, it bears repeating that **life is all about the journey**. Leaving ourselves completely open to any opportunities which come our way, ready to go with our gut feeling or intuition to see just where saying YES might take us.

Rationally second-guessing the whole route to our destination is ultimately a self-defeating exercise. Knowing where we want to arrive is clearly essential – the wonderful unpredictability of whatever will unfold taking us to getting there, and recognising these opportunities through using our intuition, is for sure the most exciting bit.

Remaining open and flexible enough to adapt to unexpected opportunities is the maximum approach to empowered living.

My first business venture for myself was a wholesale company selling to the alternative gift industry across the UK, some other areas of Europe and Canada. What became apparent over the course of running the business for a while is that no trade magazine existed for our industry. With a background in publishing I said YES to creating such a magazine to help gift shops find myself and fellow wholesalers. Producing and editing the magazine put me in touch with several brilliant new trade contacts, which rather usefully helped my wholesale business to thrive even more. Eventually as the internet started to become most gift shops primary resource, I stopped producing the magazine, but did not take the obvious step of going online with it. I believe we need to 100% follow our passions, the prospect of running an online directory failed to excite me.

What did happen though resulting from my time spent running my own publishing house, alongside the wholesale business, is it placed me in direct contact with countless high-level media contacts. When I eventually turned full time with writing and public speaking based around my writing, there I already had a ready-placed arena to raise my profile. Usually for free or a writer's fee, I have to tell you getting paid to be noticed felt amazing! All of which quickly grabbed the attention of those very people I sought to help.

Did I plan all this our beforehand? How could I foresee when I started my wholesale company that I would end up writing articles for magazines across the world to help so many people transform their lives for the better?

Giving of ourselves to others, as in my example by starting a wholesale magazine to help fellow businesses thrive by reaching their perfect marketplace, ensures we also thrive. Giving of our time, knowledge, experience, and energy pays dividends right back into our own life. In fact, giving out into the world more than we take is a simple yet profound wisdom to adopt and play forward into our daily lives.

Helping others is the surest method to allay our own misgivings or fears. Especially relevant if contemplating doing something new and outside of comfort zones, as I once did mentoring those fellow first-time performance poets. My own misgivings completely forgotten through helping others feel more at ease. Offering reassurance to someone else going through the same process makes us feel far more at empowered ourselves. This is one you need to experience to fully comprehend, helping others helps yourself.

Next time you find yourself in a stressful situation look around and see if you can offer support to anyone else going through stress. Be that shoulder for them to lean on, you will notice that you soon begin to feel a shift in your own perspective about your own challenges.

I have the habit of immediately saying YES if it feels right, this has taken me far and will do the same for YOU.

This is what led to me running the lucrative car-washing business at fourteen years old I alluded to earlier in the book. A neighbour suffered from a migraine, with her dirty car parked on the driveway I took pity on her discomfort and offered to wash it for her. Fast-forward a little to the end result of half the rest of the neighbourhood relying upon my services each week to keep their cars clean. Had I planned this beforehand? Nope, I was only being neighbourly to help someone out; yet found myself quite happy to say YES to all the other neighbours who liked the job I had done, and that extra cash proved pretty handy as well!

Having a clear concept of where we are heading is vital, an inner vision of how our life looks in terms of when we get there needs to be treasured. Achievable goals which stretch us are a goldmine.

What also needs to be treasured though are those opportunities which for sure will unfold during the journey. And we never need to know beforehand how every single step will play-out, what we do need to be though is flexible enough to adapt and happy to say YES when the time for action arrives. And it always does.

Everything I share with you through either this book or in my live talks comes from direct experiences, either stories of those I have met or from my own journey. I strongly believe we can all benefit from one another's experiences. Inner wisdom is turbo-charged when we develop the capacity to absorb learning opportunities not only from our own lives, but usefully from the experiences of other people, equipping us with an increasingly greater catalogue of options to avoiding potential pitfalls and power our way to success!

Saying YES to unexpected offers can take us somewhere we would have surely never even contemplated going before...

It never ceases to astound me how one door opening before us and saying YES, can rapidly take us off on the most fascinating and wonderful journey of personal growth. We would miss out on the thrill of all these life changing adventures if we rigidly stuck to the way we had planned it all out before.

The usefulness of a cup is in the fact it is empty, we can adopt the same attitude to learning.

It is essential to be open enough to any new opportunities and flexible enough to take necessary action when we spot those chances to do something new. Learning to trust in our intuition, instead of attempting to logically pre-plan every step, is one of the most vital skills needed to live on our terms and enjoy some fun along the way!

Do Plan This Though

It can be all too easy to find excuses to talk ourselves out of the life we deserve. Planning for sure does come in useful here firstly in terms of getting started and later keeping up the momentum.

So, what does your ideal lifestyle look like? What do you identify with as your perfect career choice? Think it might be impossible to get there? Think again!

- Does it require qualifications you do not already have? You will not have the time to study? Take evening classes at a local College or University. If this is not practical instead opt to enrol for an online qualification which need only take a few hours a week out of your time. You might have to re-arrange your schedule to fit all the study in, in all honesty so what? It is always worth the temporary inconvenience or effort of re-scheduling one area of our calendar for all the long-term brilliance a new qualification will bring into our lives.
- Is experience needed? Ask if it is possible to observe or work in a voluntary unpaid capacity part-time to gain experience. A friend did this at a whole-food café and gained a wealth of experience in the functioning of such a type of business. Now he is well on his way to starting his own similar enterprise in another town.

It is easy to come up with a thousand and one excuses to not make that first move. You know what? The time is never right if you keep on thinking it isn't!

Take that first step now. Remember you really do not need to know where the next step is, it will soon become crystal clear where and when the time has arrived to move things forward on to that second and then third step. It always is!

Start From Where You Are

Whatever your starting point in life, the desire to improve your reality takes only passion, investing some love, and the drive to make it happen. The Universe does not care if we come from a family of twelve children with parents who struggled to put food on the table or were born into the most privileged of circumstances – background is completely unimportant when daily living goals.

Having the clearest vision of where we are going, being awake to opportunity, we ensure we are going to we arrive. Energy is energy and works in thankfully the same way for us all.

Laying The Foundations

Our direction in life can change in a moment. Something we read, experience, or even dream powerfully ensures we continue from that moment with a new paradigm.

Yet for all those eureka moments which re-shape our standards of expectation from life, there can also be those even more dramatic crisis points, where we have absolutely had enough of living one way and refuse to ever put up with limitation anymore.

Out of the blue Ian found himself in possession of fifty thousand pounds as an inheritance he certainly never anticipated coming his way. For years Ian had struggled to get by financially, gaining low-skilled minimum wage employment only to then find himself quickly out of a job once more. This being largely due to his destructive lack of self-confidence in his ability to hold down a significant job. And this pattern had been going around and around in circles for most of his adult life. A self-fulfilling prophecy in action.

Ian loved gadgets and tech. Within six months of this unexpected windfall he had already blown a cool forty-five thousand of it on all the electronic gizmos he never had access to before - yet he found his life no nearer to fulfilling him.

He despaired over the prospect of the bleak winter ahead of him, and the all too real likelihood of needing to sell off many of his new toys to pay for the essentials of day-to-day living.

Having experienced for the first time in his life what it felt like to enjoy the freedom of choice, Ian developed an all-consuming passionate need for his life to never fall back into the same old routine. As he said to me "whatever it takes to avoid that pain I'll do it!" this mindset helped us to turn things around for him.

Still possessing five thousand pounds we went through ways he might invest some of this to now add some real long-term value to his employability. Raising his personal standards of expectation to build a lasting future career by improving his marketability out there in the job market.

Off Ian went to his local college for the next four months taking an intensive business management course, adding to his skills set. This was his first venture back into education since leaving high school just over a decade before with his less than average level exam passes. This course came in at slightly under two thousand pounds, leaving him three thousand left over to live off while he studied.

With the powerful motivation of avoiding the pain of ever falling back into his old life, naturally he gained his diploma. And usefully still had a little cash left over in the bank. We worked together on a new CV for him, asking about his hobbies Ian mumbled to me slightly embarrassed "just playing computer games" which we then spun onto his sparkling new CV as, "I enjoy studying IT in my spare time"!

Armed with his brilliant new qualification, kick-ass CV and far more importantly a newfound inner confidence, he commenced applying for the kind of jobs he had never even contemplated looking at before. And promptly gained permanent employment as part of the buying team for a supermarket chain. By realizing where he was heading (straight back into his old reality) Ian invested some of his remaining cash into building his knowledge base to become worth far more to potential employers.

Valuing Yourself Opens Doors

It is how we value ourselves, our personal idea of how much our knowledge and uniqueness are worth, that determines the results we get from life.

I left school at sixteen with a vague idea I wanted to work in publishing, no real plan at this point in my life, just that as a lover of books the process of publishing kind of interested me in a general way. The first company I joined happened to be the largest in town, working for them quickly failed to awaken much passion in me at all. My role seemed to be making tea and stacking shelves in the storeroom. I was learning nothing there. Yes, for sure I was only sixteen, but I still felt I was worth more than the value this company placed on my potential skills.

I lasted out a few dull weeks and moved on to a far smaller commercial publishing house. Here I was thrown right in at the deep end straight away to see if I would swim. Pitching to potential clients on the phone within an hour of arriving for work on my first day. Now this might not be the conventional route of training a still wet-behind-the-ears sixteen-year-old in business. It worked though. Although I still earning the same starting wage, I now felt valued.

I loved this job and once I overcame the nerves holding me back in those first few weeks I thrived. Even with my lack of experience, because I felt appreciated and valued, I started to look around for possibilities where I might add value to the job, the company.

Of course, my big opportunity came when the manager of the contracts department I worked in left to pursue his own dream to be a lawyer. I found myself really swimming in the deep end when at eighteen years old I got offered a three-month probationary period to see if I could run the department. Well, okay the department had only consisted of the two of us, so in a sense I was now my own manager, anyway I was impressively titled the Acting

Manager of Contracts (I even had the business card to prove it!).

Long story short, in eighteen months I brought an unprecedented million pounds worth of new business into the company slightly before my twentieth birthday, while still a teenager. Doubling the turn-over of the company in the process.

With no real experience to fall back on I had nothing to lose so I just went out and had some fun. Stretching myself and yes for sure adding a lot of value to the company, but way more importantly I proved to myself what I am truly capable of.

We are all capable of way more than we ever imagined possible and all that untapped potential is waiting right there within us ready to be released!

Did everything go smoothly? Was every day perfect? Of course not. For sure I had my learning opportunities along the way, some might label them mistakes, they only become a mistake if we keep on repeating them and do not learn to do things differently next time.

I found myself at nineteen years old earning more than five times my wages of just two years earlier. How? Certainly not by working harder or longer hours than before. I was paid for results, so I focused all my attention on the major ways to quickly get spectacular results. Here I was this teenager earning more than everyone else in the company apart from the managing director. Why? I knew I could and then went ahead to prove it!

It is how we value ourselves, our self-worth that brings results in our lives. With the right mindset we can easily become happier or more successful, and preferably both.

Mindsets Of Opportunity

Ever since she could remember Polly possessed a passionate drive for where she wanted to be as a young adult. Her goal throughout childhood had consistently been to go specifically to Oxford University to study Classics, get her degree, then continuing on all the way through further education to eventually become a professor herself and lecture at Oxford. Her entire journey through school and college was constantly motivated by her burning desire to gain the highest grades achievable to earn that place at Oxford.

Polly naturally achieved those amazing grades. Oxford now seemed but a short step away. She applied as early as possible for the course she knew she had always wanted and waited. The letter duly arrived, and Polly found she had been rejected. There had been many applicants that year and she had missed out.

How to react now?

Well, I suppose the first choice for many would be to sink into a deep depression at the rejection and throw in the towel to settle for less. Lower their standards, their expectations.

Polly did not go for this option, after the initial shock wore off, instead she saw an opportunity. She still had time on her side. Immediately she applied to Cambridge University for their course which perfectly mirrored the path her original education at Oxford would have taken. Again the letter arrived and this time she got accepted for her course!

Looking back now Polly can see exactly why she ended up at Cambridge rather than Oxford. Firstly, she adored experiencing the city whilst a student and still feels the same love for Cambridge living in her own home there in the city after over twenty years being based there. More than that though, her lecturer was so much more inclusive than she might have dreamt of. Having recognised their shared passion for Classics, he personally mentored her and went out of his way to encourage her journey to eventually getting her professorship to become a fellow lecturer alongside him. Oh, and if that is not enough, she also met a fellow student who was destined to become her future husband, all while studying right there in Cambridge!

Had her life gone along her original route, none of this future would have happened. Polly stayed true to her vision about what she wanted but adapted to see another opportunity rather than giving up her personal power by feeling rejected. She saw it in the context of what it really was, an opportunity to do something different instead.

It really is all about how we look at life that determines what kind experiences we will have. Polly chose to see plenty of things to look forward to and enjoy.

Maintaining our personal power, is about learning to react in a different way. Rather than giving up on our goals by feeling sorry for ourselves or pointlessly ranting when an apparent obstacle stands in our way, choose to take a lateral look at the situation instead. Look at what is occurring and attempt to see if there could be a positive spin to the situation. Will there be some long-term awesomeness arising from this short-term inconvenience?

Rather than focusing purely on the apparent lemon that life threw us, instead we vitally need to cultivate the habit of seeing the bigger picture and the possible uses for that lemon.

If there was only one self-empowering mindset which I could impress into the subconscious of every one of you who reads this book – determination and being open to new opportunities absolutely ensures you will succeed, whatever! Our path through life is seldom straight, adaptability to new opportunities guarantees you will arrive at your goals sooner or later.

Power and being empowered has precious little to do with the traditional image of the aggressive warrior winning out against the world. It is our own quiet inner strength which wins-out every single time. No fuss, just getting on and doing it one step at a time.

What Is The First Step To This Amazing New Life?

Deciding what it is we genuinely want!

Yet surely all of us desire above anything else to be happier, don't we?

Well...that all depends.

Unhelpful internal programming from the past still running on a loop through our decision making and influencing our choices can block us from achieving all we already possess the latent potential for.

If someone grew up in a home where parents always struggled with cash and as a child, they witnessed their friends getting cool presents for birthdays and they didn't; whichever way you look at it this person is going to have a few issues relating to money to overcome on their own personal road to success.

If you have a bad track record with making and keeping money what were your experiences growing up? What did your parents say when you wanted something in a shop that you could not have? If it something along the lines of "we can't afford that" or "there isn't enough money to buy you things all the time" it could well have set up feelings of anxiety around money. There will be never enough for everything, creating a kind of poor mentality self-fulfilling prophecy.

Parents naturally never mean to do this, they are just striving to making ends meet and once you are living your goals you can help them financially anyway if you choose, plus your own life is also going to be an example to all of your family and friends of what it's possible to achieve. More of which as we continue our journey together.

For the moment though, let us get back to this **what do you really want?** question.

It is all down to what success means to you. To some this is going to be limitless amounts of cash, to others the freedom to do what they want without having to think about budgeting for it.

Many (like your friendly author) have their personal concept of success as helping others realise their own potential, while being healthily stress-free; and all that combined together with possessing the financial freedom to able to afford to do more or less anything they wish.

Take some time to do this, ponder deeply about what you really want and that is half the trick complete.

Taking control of our own future can be our choice at any time in our lives - all it requires is making the decision to empower ourselves and giving life 100%.

The next chapter will help...

Defining Success

Success can be basically broken down into waking each morning looking forward to the day and going to bed at night feeling satisfied with what we did in-between!

The actual nuts and bolts how this success literally looks though is incredibly personal to every single one of us. We will each have our own unique vision of the kind of life we would love to lead if offered the freedom of opportunity to take it.

Success being many things to many people. Let us take some moments to define just what being successful means to us personally:

1. For some of us this will be doing exactly what we love every day and getting paid to do so, the actual amount of money is irrelevant, so long as we can pay our way, all is good.

2. We could think it terms of a financially rich lifestyle, freedom to perhaps travel or live somewhere we always wished to go. A rich lifestyle in this context is not necessarily about literally possessing

millions; it is more about being able to comfortably do everything we wish to and having the freedom of choice.

3. Or success can mean us absolutely having millions in the bank, ten houses, a helicopter, our own private island and a Mercedes-Benz in every colour of the rainbow.

4. Alternatively, success may equally be living off the grid in a hand-crafted hut, surviving off the land and rejecting the concept of money all together!

5. Or living a campervan touring Australia and writing a travel vlog on the way.

6. And even something that nobody else might have even thought of doing yet.

Ponder deeply as you focus all your attention on your perfect utopia, the perfect vision of your own life as you have always dreamt it ought to be. Daydream a little and be honest with yourself here. You deserve to take some time over this, like many of us you may well have spent many years never feeling quite satisfied with how your life is playing out.

You deserve take the time to plan out a different paradigm, however long that might take to become clear to you.

It took me over three years of unravelling the complexities of my business life (having been running two quite attention demanding businesses) to even arrive at the start of my journey into full time writing and talks. Yet once I made that 100% commitment, countless opportunities unfolded before me making the process palpably easier. And it will be the same for you once you align with your authentic self.

There are no rules when it comes to where our life can go and isn't that rather awesome? Nobody said everyone's ideal concept of success needs to be the same…find yours and that is what you align your lifestyle with to live!

Knowing When To Quit

Sometimes you have got to know when to quit, turn away from a particular journey and close the chapter in the most painless way. Some businesses have simply run their course and the industry quite literally no longer exists – an example of this is the trade magazine publishing I got involved with back in the day, the emergence of the internet as most trader's primary source of purchasing rendered paper trade publications entirely obsolete.

The same principle applies if we are employed by someone else. If the prospect of getting-up each morning is kind of dreaded as it means yet another day of doing something we fail to buy-into or feel the joy for...then it is time for a long overdue career change.

The next chapter will help you discover your own ideal career pathway to success, how essential it is to be able to mine your own unique set of talents...

Aligning With Your Talents

What separates all those stand-out high-achievers from any walk of life from the rest of the populous isn't that they are amazingly luckier or indeed extra talented, these people have recognised what they excel at and then gone right ahead to mine it. More importantly they are usually also fully aware of those areas where they lack talent and rather than wasting energy on any areas outside of their skill set, they wisely decided instead to make a career of working with what they can do.

In Harmony Or Not

What if parts of your skill set are not in harmony to your talent, for example you might be an amazing actor but lacking a commercial mindset haven't got a clue how to make this pay. Then it is time to form a mutually beneficial partnership with a person or organisation you trust who can help you achieve all you have the potential to bring into your life.

This story illustrates the point perfectly, the time I happily helped a struggling artist...

Raine is the most extraordinary of talents, her style is graphic fantasy art inspired by mythology. The first time I came across her she had entered an arts café (where I happened to be enjoying a sage tea) to see if they might display her work then she could have a chance of selling some. I have to say, impressed as I was by her artwork, Raine herself was not one of life's natural salespeople. As she proceeded to modestly sell her talent far too short and to my mind dramatically undervalue her vivid art. I seriously had to restrain myself from jumping in to stop her from talking. Instead I gave her my card and suggested I might be able to help.

Thankfully she contacted me. Putting her in touch with some prestige art galleries took her work into an entirely different arena. The proprietors loved her art as much as I did. Remarkably quickly she found herself making a great living from her creative endeavours. Her newfound confidence, after these owners of high-end galleries validated that she paints beautifully and with their customers craving more of her paintings, enables Raine to ask and receive quite frequently well over ten times the price from where she had previously valued her art.

There is always a way and if you do personally lack some of the skills which will enable you to fly, then you need to actively seek out a partnership with someone who will compliment your talents. Local networking is an excellent place to start. Is there a Chamber of Trade or Commerce in your area? Or are there meeting places or business clubs for those who, like yourself, are also starting out in a new direction with their career or seeking to grow within their existing work choice? Skill sharing is happily growing as a phenomenon. Through networking either online or in person you can find exactly what or who you need.

Stepping Off The Treadmill

So maybe you never really gave much thought about how your ideal career looks? Perhaps school was not your ideal environment and you were pleased to finally get out of the place into the world of any kind of work.

Did your job happen out of a desire for a safe option or was it because you were keeping alive a family tradition within a certain career choice? Are you working in a career solely because your parents or careers advisors at school thought it would fit you?

Perhaps you are one of those individuals who enjoys being within academia, yet now realises it is fast approaching time to spread your wings, getting out there into the arena of work.

If you fit any of these categorises or indeed even if you do not, yet lack any sense of real direction, how about finding a career path to truly satisfy you? One you will finally be delighted to pursue, making you look forward to each new day.

Sound good? Let's do this!

What Is Outside Your Skillset?

You are going to need a good old-fashioned journalist's notebook and a pen. Please use this method rather than being tempted to type on your computer or phone. There is good reason for me asking you to do it this way, information is easier for your or I to retain if physically written down old school, rather than typed.

Find a place where you are unlikely to be disturbed and start to write a list. This list is going to consist of all the things you know for sure are **outside of your own personal skill set**.

Be careful here as it can be tempting to make this an excuse list for why never having to leave comfort zones. No, on the contrary this list is all about those things which, no matter if you went to University for millennia, you would still never be able to master. It is all about getting to know yourself better and the easiest way to concentrate all our energy into those things **we can do**, is to firstly know exactly what we can't...

To start you off, here is a list of a few things outside of my own skill set:

1. Trivial pointless small talk, such as about the weather or how well (or not) a sports team might currently be doing leaves me looking blankly at the other person.

2. The finer details of business administration bores me enough to take a short nap. Although I obviously understand all the minutiae of admin tasks that come as part and parcel of running any kind of business, thankfully I have always ensured I surround myself with others who enjoy that stuff to pass these tasks along to and let them take care of them for me.

3. Dancing in a way which doesn't look comical.

4. Having much kind of empathy for lazy people or habitual excuse makers. I have had some variation

on this one said to me many times over the years "it's not my fault I didn't arrive on time, there was too much traffic" leads one to wonder why a) they didn't check the traffic situation beforehand and if it looked busy set off a little earlier and b) why they didn't phone their client (me) to let them know they were running a little late. Excuse makers make themselves difficult to employ.

5. Playing most ball games, I view sport as usually requiring wheels and an engine of some kind. I particularly love the development of eco-conscious electric powered racing cars and motorbikes.

6. Buying into the routine of doing the same thing day in and day out makes me quickly lose interest.

7. Playing the guitar. After many years on and off attempting to learn I was eventually forced to concede that playing the guitar is just not my thing and I should stick to keyboards.

There are obviously other things I cannot do, and your list will more than likely look completely different than mine. Thankfully, I can call on other people to fill in the more vital blanks in my own talents.

Do not be too hard on yourself and if you are so inclined feel free to inject a little humour into your answers, but for sure be honest. There is every reason to take time over this process, as it will be helping YOU first and foremost.

What Can You Do?

When you are done it is time to write a fresh list on a new page.

This time I want you to write down twelve of your **Emotional Assets, those individual personal qualities you know you possess.** This is not a time for modesty, allow yourself to get really carried away in this exercise. Do not think rationally too much here, just let yourself be free to automatically write.

Some of your Emotional Assets list might be:

1. Patience.
2. A sense of humour.
3. Kindness and/or empathy.
4. Great amounts of concentration.
5. Creativity.
6. Excellent ability in communication.
7. Motivating others.
8. Compelling writing.
9. Practicality.

10. Good in a crisis.
11. Studious.
12. Understanding of numbers.

Take a little time to study your two lists.

Then put aside your first Skill- Lacking list. It is necessary to go through the process of writing it to understand yourself more clearly. Now it has done its job it ceases to be relevant to your immediate future; other than offering a warning for any of us to heed regarding an attempt to build a potential career around those things which we cannot actually do! This might sound all too obvious, for sure though I have met plenty of unhappy people attempting to metaphorically fit a square peg into a round hole through pursuing a career choice they are woefully unsuited for.

The important list for now is the one which details your own Emotional Assets. This is the one to focus on.

Your life is about to get a whole lot more interesting...

Getting To Know Yourself Better

Back to your notepad and a new page to write one more final list.

This list consists of twelve things you either **personally enjoy doing or you know you would love to do given the opportunity.**

These Personal Enjoyment options can be absolutely anything at all:

1. Playing a sport.
2. Reading.
3. Public speaking.
4. Enjoying walking in nature.
5. Making clothes.
6. Driving and/or travelling.
7. Painting.
8. Singing in the shower.
9. Politics.
10. Gardening.
11. Woodworking.
12. Cooking.

Putting It All Together

Let us next make some sense of all this and see how we can now use this information to help ourselves.

Take some time to cross out all those things on your Emotional Asset list which do not represent the very

essence of who you know you are, leaving yourself only three entries.

Those parts of the myriad of qualities making up who you are which stand out as the top three things you know are positively powerfully true to you (if it helps ask someone who knows you well, you can trust to give an honest opinion with this process).

Your Personal Enjoyment list comes next. This time cross off any less important secondary interests. Leave yourself again only the top three things you know for sure you consistently enjoy or know you would love to do given the opportunity.

You will now have your two lists, along with a bit of a mess made with all those crossings-out!

Taking a fresh page write the three remaining entries from each list in two parallel lines across the top of the page.

Which could potentially read something like this...

Top Three Emotional Assets
Excellent Communication, Studious, Compelling Writing,
Top Three Personal Enjoyments
Walking in Nature, Making Clothes, Politics

On this page, underneath these lines, make a brand-new list of any possible careers which can combine at least one Emotional Asset with one of your Personal Enjoyments.

Getting paid to do what we would do anyway has to be as close to authentic living as we could ever hope to desire, let's see how to make this all real for you.

Five examples each follow based on the above Top Three Emotional Assets allied to Top Three Personal Enjoyments, obviously yours will look completely different to these examples, this is purely to help get you started:

EXCELLENT COMMUNICATION and WALKING IN NATURE
1 National park ranger.
2 Camping equipment salesperson.
3 Tourist guide taking people out into wilderness areas.
4 Cartographer.
5 Spokesperson for a green or environmental organisation.

STUDIOUS and MAKING CLOTHES
1 Formally study fashion at Uni or College for a degree.
2 Sell clothes through a local boutique.
3 Set-up a home business showing others how to make clothes.
4 Have an e-shop to sell direct to the public worldwide.
5 Start a co-operative with other craft persons to open a craft centre.

COMPELLING WRITING and POLITICS

1 Formally study journalism, become a political columnist.

2 Write campaign literature for a political party.

3 Stand to be a local councillor.

4 Aim even higher to stand as a national level politician.

5 Run a high-profile blog/vlog centred on politics with millions of avid followers.

Taking the time to do this exercise gifts us the finest chance to finally work within a career we find satisfying in every possible way. It is worth taking care to answer as honestly as we can, as this affords us the greatest opportunity to set ourselves free to experience the sheer joy of working within our personal labour of love!

Jettison The Back-Up Plans

We do not need a back-up plan, just resolute commitment and determined persistence...

I had been just as willing to buy into this as most of us are. This is one major learning opportunity for all of us and completely transformed my life once I opted out of this mindset of limitation.

We come up with a brilliant, inspirational idea – one we can buy-into on every level and immediately start looking for ways to make it happen, for it to manifest for real in our life. Yet, at the back of our mind we think "yeah, but what will I do if this doesn't work out?"

So we come up with a back-up plan for if it all fails.

If our goals are worth committing to, they are surely deserving of a 100% commitment. We do ourselves a massive disservice if at the back of our minds all the while we are thinking "well, you know, if this doesn't work out, I'll just go with whatever else" This mindset sets us up for failure every time!

Forget about back-up plans...mindfully commit to exactly what you are pursuing right now and give over all your attention on making it work for you.

Leave yourself with no choice but to commit and then whatever occurs to impede your progress (it is how we learn and grow) you are going to find a way around, over or under that hurdle. We can only develop a persistent success-centred mindset by forgetting about potential failure to kick-out forever that back-up plan!

Being adaptable within wherever we are heading on our journey is essential...to ensure we get wherever we want by utilizing all the feedback from our experiences as our own satellite navigation...constantly refining and adjusting our course until we arrive at our destination.

That is why it is incredibly important, before even beginning our journey, to at least have some idea of where we are actually heading!

Those routes to getting there play out and evolve as we travel towards goals, which is a different matter altogether and the exiting part of this journey we have chosen.

It is extremely useful to keep at the forefront of your mind when thinking about the future you are shaping for yourself <u>this or something even better</u>!

Then your plans can evolve to grab any unexpected new opportunities which present themselves.

Imagine waking each morning full of excitement for the coming day, loving how you spend your working hours and chilling in the evening feeling deeply satisfied when looking back over the happenings of the day. Sound good?

See What You Have Already Got

The true path is still to look deep within. All answers already known.

The very career you would be thrilled to be engaged in right now might be hiding in plain sight!

This takes the Aligning With Your Talents exercise we undertook a couple of chapters ago a little bit further way out there somewhere!

Take a few moments to allow yourself another sidelong glance at what you love to do and see if any possible career lays there waiting in plain sight, one which you might never have noticed before.

Pete spent all his spare time engrossed in photography. He worked in sales, he was good as well and usually topped the monthly charts at the company he worked for. It never really crossed his mind to do anything other than sales, after all it paid for his quite rich lifestyle. He came to my attention after the company he worked for ceased to exist, having been bought out by a mega-corporation with their own established sales team, Pete found himself quite unexpectedly made redundant. Although he might easily apply for and get another sales job, this abrupt interruption to his well-established routine served as a clarion wake-up call. And as he was now already in his mid-thirties, inevitably he wondered where he might be career wise when he hit forty. Whichever way he considered his future, sales was for sure not the job he wanted to be doing for the rest of his working life.

We looked around at other possible options for him. Asking him his favourite way to spend his down-time, he replied playing tennis and photography. And Pete then continuously enthused for well over fifteen minutes (barely pausing for breath!) about some of his photographs having already been published in several glossy magazines.

These lightbulb moments really do happen sometimes! We looked at one another and Pete burst out laughing. Right there hiding in plain sight was his future career. He already had a great portfolio of some high-end published work, with his sales-drive all he needed to do was search through the many thousands of photographs in his archive matching them up to suitable potential magazines and go right ahead to pitch to get them in there.

Did he make it a success? You bet he did and more importantly Pete tells me he is happier than at any other time in his life. And still enjoys his rich lifestyle.

The Student Of Life

If we are to live authentically then we need to absorb every learning opportunity at our disposal to nurture trust in our own intuition. Developing an unshakeable inner confidence to carve out our individual path...increase our value to the world.

It is extremely useful for us to reinforce this process by getting to know what makes fellow self-made successful people tick. Getting metaphorically inside their heads to discover how and why their mindset is so radically different from everyone else. Those who have been there and done that...especially useful if this also happens to be within whatever area represents our own personal passion. Their success mindset then becomes an invaluable tool for us to utilize.

We can empower ourselves by devouring autobiographies, watching vlogs or listening to audios, studying interviews online or in paper magazines and even those TV shows where members of the public pitch to business entrepreneurs. Learn for yourself what inspires and motivates these walking success stories. Find out why they get out of bed each morning. How they direct their energies and what they give attention to all day.

Take the opportunity you are given here to imprint for yourself the mindset of those already walking their talk within your area of interest. To obviously still be uniquely yourself, but consistently mirroring what you need within your actual daily focus to turbo-charge your goals and make them far more likely to happen sooner rather than later!

You can choose to replicate for yourself the mindset of any of the high achievers in whatever area interests you. This is never about giving-up on being you, it is instead about empowering yourself by utilizing other people's experience; especially useful if you have yet to have any real business experience of your own.

And you know what? 99.9% of all these high achievers we admire will have done exactly the same as you are when they started out. Including your friendly author!

Over the course of many decades I have devoured the information from more motivational, psychology and business books than I can count, watched many thousands of hours of personally inspirational vids, firstly the old-fashioned way and then later online; and I still take care to do this for at least an hour each day. I listen to audiobooks while sat at my desk or travelling in my car. This self-empowering routine is how I ended up stood talking in front of thousands of people, on radio shows/tv and writing books to help others find their path to whatever their own concept of living an amazing life might be.

Do your groundwork and you are way ahead of all those who passively wait around for their lives to change…

The Risks Worth Taking

Being prepared to take a calculated risk is a major part of the key to success. Following that inspired idea with some action. This might be massive action or just a tiny step, the point is to at least commit to doing something. This first commitment, combined with the self-discipline to see those plans right through to brilliant conclusion, ensures we are on our way!

I have started a few businesses over the years and for sure not every single one has panned out as I would have ideally preferred but that's called learning and I know the responsibility rests entirely with me for not having always given due attention to the frankly often quite obvious clues before me.

It is quite reassuring to know that virtually every active participator in life will have gone through similar learning experiences at least once and more typically several times during their careers. The trick here is to carry on anyway, straight on to the next opportunity and with a little bit more wisdom on how to *not do something* now handily stored away.

Find Your Motivational Statement

I believe we each have a mission in life, the one thing we are meant to do which is our role to fulfil in this world.

Okay, to give you the complete picture, this can change throughout our life and it is possible that what is our mission in one decade could evolve into something entirely different a little further down our timeline – but for now let's work on finding your current primary mission in life. You need to be able to sum this up on one short easy to remember statement.

This is mine: -

We all possess untold hidden talents. My role is to help others who are ready to discover theirs.

This is how I live; all my daily actions take me further towards realizing and fulfilling my mission.

Give some real thought to your own motivational mission statement, this matters precisely because it will define you. Have it as the home-screen on your phone/computer, print it out and keep a copy in your wallet or purse, leave yourself post-its where you will see them often and you might even like to actually keep a card with your mission statement written on right there above your bed taped to the ceiling. Anywhere you are going to see it often.

Your Motivational Mission Statement needs to be highly memorable to you – to embody you. Then repeat it as a mantra until it positively seeps from your pores, as you absolutely live and breathe it!

Your amazing new future could be closer than you think...

Asking For What We Want and Getting Out Of Our Own Way

Asking creates self-empowered opportunities to help us realise goals. Mutually beneficial win/win networking is a wonderful way of opening new doors and clearing the path to our goals soon manifesting.

The Only Way To Discover Answers Is By Being Prepared To Ask

Some of us can initially be a tad reticent when it comes to asking directly for what we want. Yet when looking for information, advice or even a job we clearly must be ready and willing to go ahead and ask some questions. We need to be prepared to go that extra mile, in fact as many miles as it takes...

By asking we need to be prepared to risk being turned away. Occasionally for sure it will play out that way, other times though incredible opportunities will arise because we were prepared to knock on a few doors metaphorically or even better still literally.

Persistence always pays dividends. Nurturing and developing the mindset of being doggedly determined to continually pleasantly ask for what we want, to carry right on until receiving the answers we seek however long it takes ensures we will get there one way or another.

I would always rather risk potentially looking silly for a moment by asking to know more about something I am unsure of than remain uninformed every single time. And others will respect us more for having the intelligence and confidence to ask - instead of watching us clearly struggling to muddle through without a clue!

Selling our own services or talents we must become our very own personal publicity seeking marketing manager. I did exactly that when finally launching forth full-time into the frankly already over-crowded marketplace of what is broadly labelled coaching. I have always believed we all possess that one thing to set us apart from the rest, give us some edge. I recognized this as my self-set global-wide mission to help as many people as possible.

I was in fact already quite a few years into my coaching journey when the way I might practically reach the global marketplace suddenly became so obvious I sincerely wondered how I had never noticed it before!

My path to greater things became utilizing all my existing high-level media contacts from my old publishing days to help raise my worldwide profile by writing articles and columns for magazines globally. A wonderful win/win as they got an editorial feature for their readers, and those self-same readers became aware of who I am.

And you can use this template to do precisely the same, go ahead to find that something which sets you apart within your own skill set and talents to give you some edge. Look within and it will be there for sure; and my hope is that you find yours considerably quicker than it took me!

What can you do to give yourself that edge?

Assuming it is already a given that you possess the self-belief in your new reality or in other words your goals manifesting for you (and if you really don't, please go now to find different goals to completely buy-into and believe!) how can you passionately get that message across to others in a prompt decisive way - meaning they will sit up to take notice of you?

If your business idea requires outside finance, ensure you come up with a far-reaching yet fundamentally realistic business plan including some fantastically engaging soundbites, rock solid projections and scrupulously accurate figures.

Alternatively, if you need to gain extra qualifications to help you in your goals examine the possibility of joining a company for a while that offers on the job training while they pay for your college course. Rather cool don't you feel to be getting a paid wage while you study without it costing you a penny? Together with happily possessing all that extra direct experience to take forward. Really a bit of a no-brainer if this concept can be made to fit within your projected future career. There are countless such companies out there - go find them and pitch to get that job!

If your desired career involves working in the arts, teaching or helping others, look at the possibility of grant funding being available either locally or nationally to help you pay the costs for studying. Go open those doors for yourself and send those emails.

Opportunities are always there to be taken, for sure though there are times when we need to create our own

inspired opportunities by hustling to make them happen for us.

I tend to look at what everyone else is doing, their frequently tried and worn-out tired methods, to go right ahead and do the polar opposite. How many writers and speakers see their role as actively being a publicity machine for their own work? It is generally accepted we employ someone else to do all that stuff for us, yet who else really has our own best interests at heart? And who else is better qualified to answer any potential questions about who we are and what we are offering? Placing myself right there as the first point of contact means when opportunities present themselves I am ready to grab them and say YES to see where they take me (and say NO to those which fail to excite me or don't sit well with me).

Hustle for yourself...turn over every stone, send those emails, network with the more experienced, knock on all those doors, set aside plenty fun thinking-outside-the-box-time seeking those far-out methods to generate ways of getting yourself where you deserve to be as quickly as possible. Ask and then ask some more.

You will be doing yourself the greatest favour by developing the self-discipline and determination to

persist, persist, persist until you get the results you desire.

Reticence never achieved a thing…asking always does!

Everybody Say Yes!

I cannot repeat this too many times or emphasize this point often enough, when a new opportunity arrives in front of you that feels right just say YES without thinking through too many of the implications.

Taking the steps to evolving within our potential inevitably leads to many incredible opportunities coming our way, with absolute certainty this will happen. It did and continues to do so for me and 99% of others I know. For sure this will naturally happen for you as well. We need to be sure to stay awake to these opportunities...

I ended up hosting my own radio show and enjoying a residency on a TV station for a while by saying YES to those leftfield opportunities which presented themselves.

Get into the mindset of saying YES to as many of these wonderful new experiences that come your way as possible, the ones which your intuition says to go for. At least to start off with. If nothing else it will greatly aid in the leaping out of comfort traps, even more than that though this is living life large and to the full.

Comfort traps and self-limiting inner conversations will not stand a chance if you cultivate the habit of saying YES without considering other options...

The strange thing about these new opportunities is quite often they bizarrely happen along when we are least expecting them. Those moments when we have experienced an especially challenging day or are feeling more than a little exhausted. Some happy chain of events occurs for us completely out of the blue and suddenly an entirely new vista opens before us. This is the time to act, especially if not particularly feeling in the mood...say YES and go do it anyway!

Opportunities are presented to be taken. It is up to us to grab them by both hands, tweak life on the nose a bit and see where the energy of saying YES can take us.

Getting Used To Saying No

It is liberating for all of us to develop the habit of saying YES when offered a chance to dramatically leave behind a comfort zone. I would encourage everyone to say YES to those opportunities which intuition tells us are ones to go for.

Yet there are times when saying NO is equally emphatically following our intuition. One empowering way is to say NO is to rejection. Opting to keep on keeping on anyway, persisting all the way until the results we desire finally happen for us.

Conventional wisdom for this kind of book would now have me list all those individuals in the public eye over the past few hundred years who carried right on to the fulfilment of their dream. Despite hundreds or even thousands of apparent rejections, they said NO to carry right on to make the next opportunity eventually happen for themselves. We all know the stories, the author of the books about a young wizard with glasses getting turned-down by publishers a few hundred times or the guy experimenting away to brighten our lives who eventually had his light-bulb moment. Instead I want to tell you about Lance…

Ever since Lance could remember he had wanted to be a make-up artist. Bringing the best out of people was his passion and he would practice make-overs on various willing family members from quite an early age. When he came close to leaving high-school, Lance personally went out to visit all the beauty salons within twenty-five miles of where he lived to ask if he might become their apprentice, while going part-time to College to formally study. To be turned down flat by every single one! They either did not have any openings or felt he wouldn't quite fit into their established team.

Lance still enrolled at College regardless of all these rejections. He came to my attention with only a few months of education left before the certainty of getting his qualification. This is when he started to despair a little about ever enjoying a career practicing something he loved.

We already knew the kind of vocation he was passionate about, now we needed to stretch Lance's goals into other possible career directions. Having already been rejected by every single beauty salon in the area, Lance sought to know how he could still make his dream happen. Starting his own business was not an option as this held no appeal to him, he just wanted to be creative and get paid for being creative. As we worked on his lists there was one of these lateral options that stood out as perfect for him and this was certainly the single prospective career choice which seriously excited him the most, got his inner mojo working. After a little research online, Lance applied for and got himself a position working as a make-up artist on a television drama series. By saying NO to rejection Lance now works in a glamourous job he enjoys so much he would seriously do for nothing and yet rather happily gets paid rather more than he would have ever earned working at a beauty salon.

These days when approaching new magazines around the world to write editorial features or columns for I typically get about 30% who say YES. Do you think I pay much attention to the other 70% who reject my offer or frequently never even bother to reply? Not for a moment. I reject their rejection to get on with writing the best articles I can for all the ones who do say YES. After all, for every ten magazines I approach I know I will always get three new ones to write for.

If you have some unique new niche product or service be discerning enough to say NO if a deal does not feel right. If you are genuinely innovating within a marketplace, be bold enough to hold out for that deal you are thrilled to say YES to instead.

Never buy into the fear of doing something different or new as an excuse to say NO. Just going to keep us right there in a comfort trap and as we have already established, that is anything but comfortable. Unless it feels so fundamentally wrong deep within it hurts, in which case give the offer a resounding NO.

Learn to say NO to what feel like offers too good to be true (which let's face it, they often turn out to be), those our instinct is screaming at us to avoid like they are poison, chances that is exactly what they are!

Having a publishing company of my own, producing the trade magazine for the alternative gift industry, led to an unsolicited offer coming my way. A guy who I had known back my old corporate days somehow found out what I was up to over ten years down the line and got in touch with a business proposition. He also had a publishing company. The deal he put on the table would see us joining forces, he would look after the advertising sales and my in-house design team would produce our publications. On the face of it a great win/win. Yet something did not feel right. The figures all stacked-up well, but my uneasy gut feeling told me to walk away. I said NO. Three months later I heard through the grapevine he had gone majorly bankrupt; had I joined forces with him chances are he might well have taken me with him.

Saying NO can be to either literally an opportunity before us which feels fundamentally wrong or instead to reject rejection to keep on keeping on.

Lance refused to give-up to still follow his goals, even after all those rejections from over twenty beauty salons, and he now works within a thoroughly fulfilling career area which he happily admits had previously never even crossed his mind.

We do not need to know all the steps required to take us where we desire to be, only hold fast to the vision of us doing our chosen job and for sure the way will become obvious in due course.

Say YES to all those outrageously awesome new experiences, no matter if they scare us a little, all is as it needs to be.

And say NO to those things which our intuition is telling us can only lead to something which is genuinely worth being scared stiff at the prospect of!

There are steps we can easily take to move so much closer to our ideal life...

Getting Out Of Our Own Way

Once we have created a few opportunities for ourselves we need to step back and let them happen. Standing over our opportunities attempting to impatiently force changes to occur in fact stops the progress in its tracks.

We simply cannot know at the beginning exactly how things will unfold and where the new direction will take us. We need to give our new paradigm space to breathe.

Stepping back allows far more amazing chances for greatness to occur for us, and of course being ready to act when the moment arrives – and you will know when that moment is upon you!

Stepping Closer To Goals

Just what are you prepared to do to help realise your goals?

In passionately pursuing any objective in life we do ourselves the greatest service if the answer to that question is **"anything at all it takes, without harming others!"** then go ahead to make good on that promise, that commitment.

The Magic Of Authentic Living

Prior to arriving at the point of storyboarding and planning what I would share and include in The Magic of Authentic Living, I firstly set out my fundamental goal for the book. This I defined as '**helping as many people around the world to live aa authentic a life as they possibly can**'. This objective clearly will never happen if nobody is even aware the book exists!

I am prepared to give as many interviews in any kind of media as it takes; offer excerpts from the book for as many magazines as requested; travel as far as required to public speak about the goals of the book and send copies for book reviews wherever they have the potential to reach readers as possible. This is the proven way I know I can turbo-charge the profile of this book. Firmly placing The Magic of Authentic Living out there into the mass collective subconscious.

Experience tells me I will be on a journey of at least two years during the realizing of this objective. And I am resolutely willing to travel, speak or share as much as necessary. Do anything at all it takes to empower my goal.

There are always actions we can take to move us a step or two nearer to our goals manifesting. Does not matter how tiny those steps are, walk enough of them and sure as anything we are going to arrive where we want to be someday. Daily actions are essential to stay on track to avoid falling into old limiting mindsets or self-defeating inner conversations.

What action can you take every single day to move closer to your goals?

1. Getting closer every day can be joining an online forum relating to your goals.

2. Sending an email to someone influential – even if for the moment it is only to introduce yourself or ask a polite question.
3. Setting aside time to read, watch or listen to something personally inspirational for at least half hour each day.
4. Creating and growing a professional social networking page or website/blog.
5. Spending enjoyable time imaging and clearly seeing your dream life.
6. Studying successful people's mindsets and beginning to mirror them within your own area of interest.
7. And prepare for success by investing in you (more of which shortly).

Or anything else relevant to your dream, you will know what you can do. Ensure you do take some action and do it each day - you can thank yourself later!

Write It Down

Have you bought yourself the diary we talked about back in Gratitude Changes Everything yet? If you haven't, now is the time to make that commitment to your future. A page a day type is the one to go for.

Each day write down at least five tasks in your diary (however small these tasks are) for yourself to act upon to help take you closer to your chosen new reality becoming your life and then be willing to carry them through to conclusion.

Ticking them off your list as completed is incredibly self-motivating helping to keep you on track. I have done this since the beginning of my career and resolutely believe this simple action has helped me reach where I am at now and will continue to enable to me to grow within my abilities to communicate to audiences and readers ways to help them personally grow.

Typically, my self-set tasks each day, listed in my own diary might read something like this:

1. Reply to any emails received in the last 24 hours.
2. Spend some time in my recording studio working on new audiobooks or music poetry albums.
3. Negotiate with potential venues for my own seminars and/or holistic event organisers for me to present talks at.
4. Study for at least an hour.

5. Check everything is going according to plan at Alive To Thrive Ltd and offer any constructive feedback to my incredible team to help them to further excel.

Developing an empowered mindset is a constant work in progress, evolving with us to carry us all the way and the journey never ends, as we shall see later. Vigilance is needed if we are to keep on track for where we desire to be. Distractions and cul-de-sacs are frequently going to be encountered.

Use these methods, enabling you to carry on moving forward. Personal mind-training exercises: buy into them, practice them often – your goals then become realistic in your subconscious mind and feel infinitely more achievable.

Inspiring Others

We have all come across those types of people who focus most of their energy on aggressively attempting to convince everyone they encounter they are the best at what they do and the only possible valid opinion worth taking on board belongs exclusively to them.

If someone genuinely is the best in their field or indeed their opinion is invariably the one to listen to, clearly this is going to be self-evident and is hardly going to require constant self-validation.

Those who repeatedly loudly proclaim to be the most wonderful thing ever are heading for a fall, might take a little while to all play-out, for sure it happens every time though. Those unfortunate people we encounter who feel the need to insufferably brag to one and all about how great they are will usually be masking issues relating to poor self-confidence and self-esteem, or else they are simply emotionally immature.

Shouty, aggressive self-validators are never a lot of fun to work alongside or hang-out with. Their conversations being focussed solely on the genius of themselves quickly wears a bit thin for everyone around them.

The truly empowered are confident in their abilities. As we have already established, successful people play to their known strengths and structure their life around how best to utilize those skills they know they possess. Rather than arrogant self-validation, they let all their actions speak for themselves for others to draw their own conclusions accordingly.

Humility Is Empowered

Humility is allowing those we mix with the right to have their opinion and naturally expecting the same courtesy in return. If we are proven to be right on an occasion, then if asked, taking care to explain how we came to what turned out to be the correct conclusion and staying on good terms with those who this time round turned out to be incorrect.

When we are later in their shoes, as nobody owns exclusive rights to be right every single time, if we can get our ego out of the way to ask them to also explain how and why they arrived at their correct conclusion, we equip ourselves with yet another empowering mindset to play forward into our own lives. Humility is win/win.

Politeness Costs Nothing

Bizarrely some people seem to believe that allowing consideration for others is to be showing some kind of weakness. Nothing could be further from the truth...

If we choose to go through life acting with due consideration for the feelings of others we need to realise, with absolute certainty, we are not always going to get things done our own way. Yet this is okay if we move aside our ego to embrace what we instead care to consider as an opportunity to learn. Through a little compromise we end up taking a direction we would never have considered venturing along otherwise. Leading forward into brilliant new adventures or discovering something radically different and exciting. Still win/win then after all, even if for now we are following someone else's plan this time.

The skills and art are knowing when the right moment is to assertively stick to our point of view and ensure our way is the way things happen; and when we need to back-off a little, happy this time to go with the flow to interestingly seeing where the situation ultimately take us.

A trend started in the West in the 1980's where suddenly politeness became unfashionable. Greed and selfishness were portrayed as being okay in the press and popular culture, through the uber-cool ruthless businesspeople portrayed in movies and television series. There is a polar difference in the energy of pleasurably pursuing our goals with love; and walking over others to achieve objectives. That kind of approach never sustains or leads to any kind of lasting happiness. Yet the hard-hitting no compromise approach today still seems attractive to many...

As one who lived through the 1980's, I can observe exactly where many of my contemporaries who engaged with a ruthlessly single-minded mindset ended up and not surprisingly remarkably few of them seem to be living exactly what could be described as happy lives. For sure, their selfish approach often ensured some material wealth came their way, yet money only counts for a small percentage of what it means to be entirely successful. What is the pleasure in living alone in an impressively lavish house if we have three acrimonious divorces behind us and grown-up children we never see? Without joy in the soul all the money in the world is not going to mean a great deal of anything much. Aggressively pursuing wealth for solely the sake of gaining wealth is a hollow victory.

By actively pursuing our goals, creating win/wins along the way by helping others, our main focus and motivation remains the dream of ours which is being passionately attained; and all the financial rewards resulting out of this process happen as a happy secondary by-product. And with this kind of energy, we will be free to enjoy our new-found financial freedom. Life is all about the journey...

We All Have The Right To Grow At Our Own Pace, How Else?

Another interesting point here is that we cannot force anyone to be who they are not or grow any faster than they are able. There have been members of my own teams throughout my several business ventures over the years who I felt would benefit from some of the plethora of opportunities for self-growth which are available to anyone and everyone who is ready. Oh boy! Let's just say we truly cannot change others and can only work on ourselves to be an example of what is possible.

After regularly buying copies of the books which personally inspired me to give as gifts to my staff, I eventually understood that although I could see how valuable this stuff was, most of those around me failed to get why they should in fact ever bother actually reading any of them!

The Desk-Thumping Approach Is So Last Century

I do hear some horror stories at seminars and through my talks; workplace bullying is apparently alive and well. The tyrant approach is unbelievably still employed be some managers even in the 21st century!

Back in the early 1990's, Lee Fraser (my father, hence the same surname!) was one of five regional sales managers in a mid-sized media type business. Every month there would be a management meeting at head office, and it was compulsory to attend.

The typical routine went something like this. The five regional managers were not allowed to drive to the meeting. After work they each would travel by late evening train to be met at the station by someone from head office and taken to hotels. Each regional manager was given a different hotel to stay in, but they all had one thing in common, no late-night dining facilities or restaurant within easy walking distance.

Meetings started early at this company; the regional managers would be expected to be ready for picking-up at 7am to be driven straight to head-office.

Before 8am they all were seated around a conference table for their monthly meeting. Having been served their choice of hot drink at the commencement of the meeting, that remained it as far as sustenance was concerned until the meeting broke at around 11am for a fifteen-minute recess. There were no vending machines or any other means of finding anything to eat or drink. The meeting reconvened and a further hot drink was served.

These were high pressure events, the managing director would shoutingly inform them that having almost met their targets he was unhappy as he must have set them far too low and proceeded to raise them higher or some other thoroughly de-motivating business plan.

This unsmiling tyrant of a managing director hadn't been at the sharp end canvassing for customers for many years and was unrealistic about competition; he was completely out of touch with his own marketplace and the regional managers all knew this. Can you imagine how much they respected his opinion?

A working lunch was served around 1pm consisting of a sandwich each. Around 4.30pm the meeting would finally close, which saw five hungry and dehydrated regional managers being duly delivered to the railway station for their home journey.

My father lasted less than six months with this company, not surprisingly they had a high turnover of staff. I think the writing was probably on the wall when he took bottled water and a packed lunch to one of their monthly meetings...

He talked at length to one of the junior directors when he handed in his resignation and explained he thought their people management skills were out of the stone-age. In all fairness the guy had to agree, he said something along the lines of the managing director feeling that keeping his managers hungry (literally apparently!) and creating the environment they were never quite sure if they would have a job from month to month would keep them on their toes and ensure they gave their most to the company cause.

Well I suppose it is a point of view, yet not a terribly effective one.

Team Building

As any empowered manager will confirm, getting the best from others requires encouragement and setting realistic targets with clear incentives once they are reached. Making staff all feel part of a team and for sure here we are collectively working towards the same cause. Trusting them with responsibility and giving them the space to get on with their tasks (but also being available if they need help). Ensuring everyone feels comfortable within their environment then work becomes a mutually pleasurable experience for all.

At some point, inevitably someone is going to make an error – a member of staff will forget to do something, inadvertently negotiate a poor deal or any of the other hundred and one crisis moments which happen in the day to day running of a business.

Having an open-door policy for staff to bring their issues to the manager is essential; our manager needs to be accessible to his or her co-workers. If the error is not down to dishonesty or downright incompetence, supporting the member of staff and helping them sort out their mess will ensure team loyalty far more than any metaphorical dragging them over hot coals. They will usually be fully aware they goofed-up and allowing them the chance to atone and make things good team builds brilliantly!

As a business owner, if a senior manager makes an error in judgement, the automatic response for many companies seems to be to let them go and replace them. Far better again, unless the error is down to dishonesty or catastrophic incompetence, back them and allow them to sort their mess out. Everyone goofs-up sometimes...if it can be fixed then support the process and if it is truly beyond repair, be honest within the company and then firefight to recover any public loss of reputation.

Acting The Part

> "All the world's a stage, and all the men and women merely players"
>
> William Shakespeare summed up life quite succinctly in this quote from As You Like It...

Children have acting as if down to a fine art. Thinking back to childhood, we all so easily role played. When we are children we can make believe we are pretty much anything or anyone and then behave accordingly to play out that accepted role...

Funnily Enough, Adult Life Is Essentially The Same!

Let's use the example of Aisha training to be a lawyer. Off she goes to University for six years to fulfil her dream. How much of the process she goes through is purely about the mechanics of learning the law and how much is also about taking on the mindset of being a lawyer?

We expect certain standards of behaviour from our legal specialists and are more likely to commission a lawyer to work for us if they act roughly within the generally accepted parameters of a lawyer. Most of us would be far less inclined to trust our important legal matters to a heavily tattooed lawyer dressed in ripped jeans and a heavy metal t-shirt, who calls us mate in every sentence; we would not feel the necessary level of trust in their ability. Aisha studies and spends her leisure time in the company of fellow law students, without consciously planning it that way, as well as learning the finer points of law she gradually takes on the mindset of being a lawyer.

We expect certain mindsets from certain professions and quite naturally feel uncomfortable when faced with someone who has personal energy and actions that are incongruous within those accepted guidelines.

This applies to any profession or pursuit. Would we go off for a week into the wilderness with the guide who forgets our name five seconds after we have told them and fails to carry any kind of navigation equipment or communication devices? Or pay to go to the theatre to see an actor who has openly declared in the press how much he hates his apparently philistine audiences.

We can do so much to help ourselves here!

Say you want to be a writer. Do your homework. Read about fellow writers. Autobiographies, blogs, magazine articles, anything at all which aids in an understanding of what makes them tick. What is the successful writer's mindset within your chosen genre? What do they do all day? How is their schedule organized?

Good start, next think of yourself **as a writer!** You are not going to be a writer one hazy day in the future after passing a degree – you **are** a writer! The fact you may yet be unpublished or are still at University is entirely irrelevant; if you have physically written something, anything at all within your chosen genre...you are a writer. Think like one!

This is my writer's mindset – I expect to get ideas for chapters and subject matter to include in my forthcoming books or magazine columns. I focus my attention on writing a lot. Whether I am walking on the beach, waking-up in the morning or having my six-monthly dental check-up...doesn't matter where I am or what I am doing. By expecting to get new ideas they constantly manifest for me.

If your dream is to be a singer, well firstly can you sing? Great, you are a singer! Next take steps to earn your pay from your singing talent. Think like a singer and seek out ways to do what you love every day. Find a manager you can trust if commercial stuff is not your thing. Literally create your dream for yourself. Tell everyone you are a singer and are looking for ways to perform. A way is inevitably about to open for you to sing for the pleasure (and pay) of others.

A reminder that it does not matter what your chosen dream career is, empower yourself by taking care to study the mindset of those already within in it and use their experience.

This is never about losing your individuality; on the contrary you are still going to be the unique personality you always were. Rather it is about gaining empowering internal programming by adopting their already successful mindset, convincing your subconscious to accept the reality of this being exactly what and who you are.

As you are projecting this mindset or energy – the wider world is also seeing you as exactly the person you desire them to accept you as, constantly reinforcing the reality.

Invest In You

To get taken seriously by others we need take our own image seriously. Like it or not others do judge by what they see. Might not always seem fair, nevertheless they always do.

Originally I thought to use the sub-heading Dress The Part here, but really that would be only a partial truth. INVEST IN YOU is more accurate as it includes wider ranging implications, rather than simply putting on a cool dress or designer suit expecting that to do the work for us. As usual there is a bit more to it than that. What matters here is creating an empowered mindset for ourselves. Those new neural pathways we are creating to hardwire our subconscious.

Feeling good about ourselves is critically important in achieving goals and for sure an important part of this process is investing in how we present ourselves to the world and how that makes us feel...

Bottom line, if you are starting out and want to get taken seriously in practically any kind of area of business it sure pays to look successful!

Wear clothes which suit the dream you are pursuing. When I first ventured out many years ago into part-time touring the more embryonic versions of what my talks later evolved into, I decided beforehand that by wearing bandanas and positively unmissable loudly patterned shirts or waistcoats I would stand out to get noticed – this worked, gaining me much appreciated free local press coverage at the time and began to place me on the map.

Thankfully for everyone else I did later moderate this through experience. And although, as I mentioned earlier, I have been labelled by the press The Hippie Holistic Coach, these days when out public speaking I do tone-down a wee bit my natural inclination to dress like a member of a 1960's psychedelic rock band who somehow time-travelled into the 2020's!

If we project successful, we are going to get taken seriously and literally become more successful...isn't that a rather awesome self-fulfilling prophecy?

Dress to impress YOU first and foremost. Ensure you feel good about your clothes, hair and personal style, then you are projecting that energy the whole time and everyone you meet happily reinforces the feel-good factor for you. Buy the best you are currently able to afford, and for sure you then will soon have more spending power as your success increases.

Model how a successful person in your chosen career dresses. Treat this as purely your starting point for inspiration, then develop your own style within this successful framework into one which is now shouting out 100% you.

After all you are the one person in the world most qualified to be you!

If you are on a limited budget consider how you allocate your spending. After you have seen to firm commitments, how can you make the rest of your money best work for you? Even if for the moment this is only amounts to a small change.

Invest any of your surplus cash into things which will add value to your life. This can take many forms including:

- Courses and further education.

- Books.

- Audio Downloads.

- Clothes for the feel-good factor.

- Trips to hear motivating talks.

- Conferences for networking.

Anything at all, however abstract or leftfield, which adds value to life and brings those precious dreams so much closer to really being real is what we need to buy-into.

Conclusion and Afterword

In these strange times.

Always looking for the signs.

Guidance along our way.

Paying heed without delay.

Signals from the Universe.

Thoughts polarity to reverse.

Negativity will depart.

When we open our heart.

Introduction

One of the most vital transformational techniques I teach is that if we want to keep ourselves on track, staying right there in the zone, it is essential to read, watch or listen to something personally inspiring each day.

The energy we put out there in the Universe, what we programme our subconscious minds with through our conscious thoughts and experiences, makes the life we lead.

Keep this central as part of your daily routine and my labour of love in writing this book will have fulfilled its mission.

Life Is Still About The Journey

We all need remember to remember this. Although the ultimate destination is wonderful, also taking the time to enjoy the process of living each day throughout the journey of getting there ensures we remain motivated to achieve ever more.

Celebrate Your Successes To Be Ready For More!

Each time you achieve some notable success...a further step towards your end game...it is time to CELEBRATE!

This can be any type of significant milestone - like passing exams, getting a step-up in your career, earning that first 10k through your own first business, quitting smoking for good or even becoming fit enough to run the New York marathon.

Whenever a significant life achievement is gained then it is time to acknowledge this and find some outrageous way to mark the occasion. One that you and everyone else will remember for a long time:

- Taking your family or friends for a fantastic night out at a top-class vegan restaurant.
- Going with your significant other for a deeply relaxing pampering weekend experience at a five-star spa or wellbeing centre.
- Or if the event is truly exceptional, booking an out of this world vacation at such an outrageous destination you and your closest will be thrilled just at the prospect of spending time there, with a departure date as soon as possible.

Celebrating needs to essentially be some event you would never have even considered prior to your new-found success.

Could be a private box at the theatre to see a Shakespeare play in Stratford-upon-Avon or a long weekend shopping experience on 5th Avenue in New York. The point is this crucially needs to be something that reinforces on so many levels how your life is different now and this event validates the proof of it!

If pays to make our own successes events everyone can enjoy, and the great energy created by family and friends joining with us to celebrate our achievements will only add to the self-fulfilling effect of yet more success waiting for us and crucially open their eyes to their own long-held dreams becoming possible.

Win/win all round then!

So, what next?

It Actually Never Finishes; Thought I Had Better Let You In On This Secret!

When you have finally seen some those long-held wellbeing and lifegoals realised, and by following the steps throughout this book you certainly stand a good chance of them finally coming to be your life, other dreams gradually organically proceed to take pride of place as future goals.

It really does never end and indeed quite right too, it truly never needs to!

All active achievers in life will constantly set themselves new challenges or targets and keep their motivation mojo going all the way through to their completion.

Once you have personally witnessed a few of those once seemingly impossible dreams come to pass in your own life, you find yourself happily in a position to stretch your expectations even further within whatever turbo-charged new goals you are able to achieve!

Then you set out once again for the next chapter of this great adventure called your life...

And remember anything you want from life that is literally physically possible in any way at all must by its nature become achievable, now here is the true essence of The Magic of Authentic Living!

Dean Fraser

About Dean Fraser

Over the last three plus decades I have worked as an artist; owned a wholesale business selling crystal healing kits, dowsing pendulums and books; had a publishing house; spent time as an antique dealer and ran an events company. I qualified in Body Language Psychology twenty five years ago. All the while during this time I have also helped people. My passion is helping others to lead fuller lives. I love standing in front of an audience ready to offer potentially life-changing new paradigms and simple transformational techniques through bringing positive energy into their lives or sharing my esoterically inclined poetry.

Books by Dean Fraser

A Healing For Gaia

Beyond Poetry

Staying Positive Regardless

The Magic Of Authentic Living

The Poems Less Spoken

Thriving!

Walking Our Talk Is Easy, Right?

The Complet
Unlock Your Life With
Pendulum Dowsing

Dean Fraser

247 Poems

Dean Fraser
THE QUANTUM POET